New York State

Science

 Continental

Acknowledgments

Illustrators: Pages 18 *ruler and balance,* 19 *thermometer and graduated cylinder,* 44, 89, 109, 110, 112, 124, 129, 133, 137, 155, 190, 199, 201, 208, 209, 211 Zeke Smith; Pages 57, 59, 60, 64, 67, 81 *bottom,* 82 *top,* 139, 140, 158, 160, 165, 171, 172, 204 John Norton; Pages 61, 86, 92, 103, 116, 193, 194, 195, 205, 210 Laurie Conley; Page 99 Cindy Shaw; Page 172 *butterfly* Estrella Hickman

Photo Credits: Front cover and title page www.istockphoto.com/zosko; Page 80 *heater* www.istockphoto.com/futureimage, *lamp* www.istockphoto.com/bmcent1, *tree* www.istockphoto.com/DNY59; Page 102 www.istockphoto.com/danielkolman; Page 105 *stratus clouds* NOAA's National Weather Service Collection, Robert F Kresge; Page 108 www.photos.com; Page 118 www.istockphoto.com/DNY59; Page 123 *metal spoon* www.istockphoto.com/KMITU, *wooden spoon* www.istockphoto.com/jcphoto; Page 124 www.istockphoto.com/gvictoria; Page 130 www.istockphoto.com/Dennis_Hammer; Page 138 www.istockphoto.com/The-Tor; Page 150 *button* www.istockphoto.com/Joss, *domino* www.istockphoto.com/JJMaree, *book* www.istockphoto.com/LukaSphoto, *frame* www.istockphoto.com/evirgen, *pocket watch* www.istockphoto.com/A.Carina; Page 155 www.istockphoto.com/RobertPlotz; Page 156 www.istockphoto.com/swilmor; Page 159 *mangrove trees* www.istockphoto.com/sumos, *deer* www.istockphoto.com/mmette; Page 161 www.photos.com; Page 162 www.istockphoto.com/PetrFlgl; Page 163 www.istockphoto.com/brm1949; Page 164 *tree* www.istockphoto.com/DNY59; Page 166 www.istockphoto.com/cunfek; Page 167 www.istockphoto.com/Scrofula; Page 168 *winter hare* www.shutterstock.com, *summer hare* Image used under GNU Licensing from Gilad.rom; Page 176 *walking stick* www.photos.com, *deer* www.istockphoto.com/cjmckendry; Page 177 Wikimedia Commons; Page 178 www.istockphoto.com/Nattesha; Page 180 *honeybee* © MzePhotos.com, *plant* www.en.wikipedia.org; Page 181 www.istockphoto.com/djwild; Page 182 www.istockphoto.com/JulieVMac; Page 183 *leaf* www.photos.com; Page 185 www.istockphotos.com/zcengerme; Page 188 U.S. Fish and Wildlife Service on USFWS/Midwest Region; Page 191 Image used under Creative Commons from Fritz Geller-Grimm; Page 192 *acorn* www.istockphoto.com/pixhook, *mature oak* www.istockphoto.com/Elenathewise, *oak seedling and sapling* www.istockphoto.com/redmal; Page 195 www.photos.com; Page 196 *maple tree* www.istockphoto.com/eas, *hummingbird* www.istockphoto.com/SteveByland; Page 206 www.photos.com; Page 213 *cows being milked* www.istockphoto.com/kickers, *dairy machine* www.istockphoto.com/Millanovic, *milk being bottled* Courtesy of California State University, Fresno, *milk in store* www.photos.com

ISBN 978-0-8454-6720-6

Table of Contents

Welcome to New York State Science

This book was written to help you get ready for the NYS Science test. You've been studying science ever since you started school. You will need to remember things you have not studied in a long time. As you get close to the test, the best way to prepare is to review the ideas and practice the skills you will need for it.

New York State Science contains lessons to review the things you have learned in science class. Each lesson includes examples to remind you what an idea means or show you how a skill is used. There are also three hands-on lessons. These lessons contain step-by-step instructions to help you practice important science skills.

On the right side of many lesson pages is a sidebar. It contains definitions of words you might not know or remember, and facts about things that are related to the main idea of the lesson. After each lesson, there are sample test questions to help you practice what you have reviewed.

The practice pages have two different kinds of questions. That's because the real New York test has two kinds of questions. The questions in this book will help you find out what you know about science skills and ideas. Just like on real science tests, some of the questions in this book will be easy for you. Others may make you think a bit. And a few will be a challenge.

- The first type of question found in this book is a **multiple-choice** question. Most of these questions give you four answers to choose from. A few questions give you only three answer choices. In each lesson of this book, there are a few sample multiple-choice questions. A box under the item tells you how to think about the question so you can find the correct answer.

  When you answer a multiple-choice question, be sure to read *all* of the answer choices carefully before choosing one. Some questions can be tricky if you do not read closely.

- The other type of question is an **open-ended** question. These questions can be correctly answered in more than one way. You must answer these questions in writing, using your own words. The answers you need to give might be very short and simple, or they might be very detailed. The box under the question will explain how to think about the question so you can answer it in your own words. Then a sample answer is given. To answer an open-ended question, follow the item instructions *exactly*. Ask yourself, "Am I answering the question that is being asked? Have I included everything I need to include, but not included information that isn't asked for?" Always think about what you will say *before* writing your explanation. Your thoughts should be clear and organized. Your writing should be neat so it is easy to read.

At the end of each lesson there are some practice questions. Usually, there will be a few multiple-choice questions and one open-ended question. These questions will help you find out how much you remember from the lesson. They will also give you practice answering questions like the ones you will see on the New York test. You should answer these questions on your own if possible, just as if you were taking the real test.

At the end of each unit there are a few pages of review questions. The questions in this section cover all the lessons in that unit, in a mixed order. The review includes both types of questions you worked with in the lessons: multiple-choice and open-ended questions.

This workbook was created to give you some practice for the NYS Science test. It will help you remember the science facts and ideas you have learned. It will give you the chance to answer the same kinds of questions you will see on the test. Good luck!

Unit 1
Analysis, Inquiry, and Design, Part 1

Scientists ask questions about the world. They look for answers by observing things. Sometimes scientists make predictions. They may design experiments to test their predictions. In this unit, you will learn how to think like a scientist. You will also practice important skills, such as measuring.

There are six lessons in this unit:

1 **Scientific Investigations** To learn about the world, scientists do scientific investigations. They may make careful observations. They may do experiments. They do these things to answer questions. In this lesson, you will learn how to ask a scientific question. You will also learn how to design a fair experiment.

2 **Math in Science** Scientists use many math skills in their investigations. In this lesson, you will learn about math skills that most scientists use every day.

3 **Collecting and Displaying Data** The information that scientists collect is called data. Scientists use tools to help them collect data. In this lesson, you will learn how to collect and record data. You will also learn about tables, graphs, and other ways of sharing data.

4 **Analyzing Data and Drawing Conclusions** When scientists analyze data, they study it to figure out what it means. Then they can draw conclusions and answer questions. In this lesson, you will learn how to use data to draw and support a conclusion.

5 **Sharing Scientific Ideas** Scientists often work together. They may help each other carry out an investigation. They may share ideas and test each other's results. In this lesson, you will learn why it is important that scientists work together. You will also learn about why it is important to be skeptical.

6 **Hands-On Lesson: Measuring** Measuring is an important scientific skill. In this hands-on lesson, you will practice measuring length, mass, and volume. You will also record and analyze data.

Scientific Investigations

Major Understandings 1S1.1a, b; 1S1.3a; 1S2.1a

Scientific **investigations** can help you learn about the world. There are many ways to do a scientific investigation. One way is to do an experiment. Many scientists do experiments. You, too, can do experiments to learn about the world.

Making Observations

All scientific investigations start with an **observation.** An observation is something you notice. You make observations using your senses. For example, you could make observations about a tree. You could notice that the tree is taller than you are. You could feel that its bark is rough. You could see that its leaves are green. You could smell the scent of its flowers.

After you make observations, you can record them to help you remember them. You can use numbers, words, or pictures. Record your observations clearly and carefully. That way, it will be easier for others to understand them.

Give <u>two</u> examples of observations you could make about a bird.

Some things you can observe about a bird are its color, its size, the shape of its beak, and what its song sounds like.

Asking Scientific Questions

Think about the last time you observed something you did not understand. You may have asked, "Why did that happen?" Scientists also ask why things happen. Scientists do scientific investigations to answer questions and learn more about the things they observe.

A **scientific question** is a question that you can answer with a scientific investigation. Scientific questions have to be very clear. You have to be able to answer them using **data.** Data are pieces of information, such as observations.

You have to answer scientific questions with facts. You cannot use an opinion to answer a scientific question. An opinion is a belief based on feelings. It cannot be proved. A fact about a walnut could be that it is 3 cm long. An opinion about a walnut could be that it is tastier than an almond.

An **investigation** is a careful study used to answer a scientific question. Many scientists do experiments. Others do not. A scientific investigation does not have to include an experiment.

You make **observations** when you see, hear, taste, smell, or touch things. Observations include measurements.

A **scientific question** is a question that can be answered using only observations.

Data are pieces of information. A single piece of data is called a *datum.*

Which of the following is most likely a scientific question?

A Which hamburger tastes the best?

B Which animal at the zoo weighs the most?

C Are purple flowers smellier than blue flowers?

D Do plants look nicer under red light or green light?

Remember that scientific questions cannot be answered with opinions. Which hamburger tastes the best, whether a flower is smelly or not, and when plants look nicest are opinions. Those questions are not scientific. The weight of an animal in a zoo is a fact. You can measure the weight of each animal. The correct choice is B.

Most scientific investigations do not start with a "why" question. That's because most "why" questions have very complicated answers. It often takes many investigations to answer them. So, scientists ask smaller, clearer questions. The answers to those questions can help them answer the "why" questions. For example, you may wonder, "Why do paper towels absorb liquid?" To help answer this question, you might ask a more specific question. You might ask, "What brand of paper towel can absorb the most water?"

Making a Prediction

After you have decided on a question to investigate, you should try to think of an answer for the question. This is called a *prediction*. For example, suppose your question is "What brand of paper towel can absorb the most water?" Your prediction could be that brand A paper towel will absorb the most water.

You should state your prediction clearly. Do not use opinion words, like *best* or *worst*. For example, "Brand A paper towels will absorb water best" is not a good prediction. It does not say what *best* means.

State your prediction so that you can test it. A better prediction is "Brand A paper towels will absorb more water than other paper towels." You can measure how much water each paper towel absorbs. Therefore, this prediction is testable.

You can compare the results of your investigation with your prediction. Do not worry if your prediction is wrong. Scientists often make predictions that are wrong. These unexpected results are very exciting. They make scientists think of new ways to explain the things they observe.

Which of the following is the best scientific prediction?

  A The plant that gets the most water will grow the tallest.

  B The plant with the best seeds will grow the highest.

  C The plant with the longest roots will grow best.

  D The plant that gets the most light will be prettiest.

> A scientific prediction must be testable. Which seeds are best and which plant is prettiest are opinions, so they cannot be tested. Choices B and D are incorrect. Choice C is also incorrect, because it does not say what *best* means. You can measure the amount of water given to a plant and how tall it grows. Therefore, the prediction in choice A is testable. The correct answer is A.

Conducting an Experiment

You can test your prediction that brand A paper towels can absorb the most water. You can use an experiment to test it. There are certain steps you should follow when you conduct an experiment.

First, identify the **variables** in the experiment. A variable is any condition that can change during an experiment. In the paper towel experiment, the variables might be the thickness of each paper towel, the size of each paper towel, the brands of paper towels tested, and how long the paper towel is in the water.

> **Variables** are the things in an experiment that can change.

When you do your experiment, you need to keep all of the variables the same except one. The variables that you keep the same are called the *controlled variables.* The variable that you change is called the *uncontrolled variable.* An experiment that has only one uncontrolled variable is called a **controlled experiment.**

It is important to control all of the variables except one. If more than one variable changes, you cannot know which variable caused what you observe during the experiment. For the paper towel experiment, you predicted that brand A paper towel will absorb the most water. Therefore, the uncontrolled variable should be the brands of paper towels you test.

> A **controlled experiment** has only one variable that changes. The others stay the same.

After you identify the variables in your experiment, list all of the **materials** you need. The materials are all the different items that you will use when you conduct the experiment. Your materials list might include:

- four paper towels that are the same size but different brands
- four measuring cups
- stopwatch
- 50 milliliters (mL) of water for each cup

Next, write out the steps you will follow. You can also make a drawing of what you will do, such as the one below.

Container #1:
Brand A towel
50 mL water

Container #2:
Brand B towel
50 mL water

Container #3:
Brand C towel
50 mL water

Container #4:
Brand D towel
50 mL water

Describe <u>six</u> steps you should follow for this experiment.

The steps might include the following:
1. Make a chart for your data. Record which brand of paper towel is in each measuring cup.
2. Pour 50 mL of water into each measuring cup.
3. Place the end of each paper towel in a measuring cup.
4. Let the towels sit in the water for 30 seconds (s).
5. Pull each paper towel out of the measuring cup and set it aside.
6. Measure the amount of liquid remaining in each cup. Record the measurement on the chart.

Before you carry out your experiment, decide what observations you will make and how you will record them. For the paper towel experiment, you could record:

- which brand of paper towel was in each cup
- how much water was in each cup before you put the paper towel in
- how long the paper towels stayed in the water
- how much water was in each cup after you took the paper towel out

You can record your observations in a table, such as the one shown below.

PAPER TOWEL EXPERIMENT

	Container #1	Container #2	Container #3	Container #4
Brand of paper towel	brand A	brand B	brand C	brand D
Amount of water in cup (start)	50 mL	50 mL	50 mL	50 mL
Amount of time towel was in cup	30 s	30 s	30 s	30 s
Amount of water in cup (end)	45 mL	42 mL	38 mL	48 mL

Other Kinds of Investigations

Not all scientific investigations are experiments. Some scientists collect data in nature. Others make computer models. Some scientists do surveys. They ask people questions and record their answers.

For example, you could do a scientific investigation about a bird you see near your school. You could carefully observe what the bird looks like and how it acts. Then, you could read books to learn about it. You could share your observations with others. All of those steps are part of scientific investigations.

It's Your Turn

Please read each question carefully. For each multiple-choice question, circle the letter of the correct response.

1 Which of the following is an example of an observation?

  A Thunder is scarier than lightning.

  B Blue jays are larger than chickadees.

  C Road bikes are better than mountain bikes.

  D Soccer is harder than baseball.

2 A student visits a local park. He observes the living things there. He thinks of a scientific question based on his observations. Which of these questions does he most likely think of?

  A Are trees prettier than grass?

  B What kind of flower smells nicest?

  C Are streams more fun than ponds?

  D What kind of tree lives the longest?

Base your answers to questions 3 and 4 on the information below and on your knowledge of science.

A student wants to do an experiment. She wants to use a golf ball, a basketball, a soccer ball, and a tennis ball. She wants to see how high each ball bounces when she drops it on a wood floor.

3 Which of the following is the best prediction for this experiment?

  A The tennis ball will bounce better than the golf ball.

  B The basketball will not bounce as well as the soccer ball.

  C The tennis ball will bounce highest.

  D The golf ball will not bounce very well.

For this open-ended question, write your answers on the lines.

4 List <u>two</u> materials that the student would need to conduct this experiment. Do not list any of the balls that the student will need.

  (1) _____

  (2) _____

Math in Science

Major Understandings 1M1.1a–c

Math is very important in science. Most scientists use math every day to do their work.

Math Skills for Scientists

Scientists ask questions about the natural world. They conduct investigations to help them answer those questions. Scientists use many math skills during investigations.

Math Skill	Key Symbols	Scientists May Use This Skill to ...
Adding	+	• Count objects • Combine measurements or other kinds of data
Subtracting	−	• Find the difference between measurements or other kinds of data
Multiplying and Dividing	×, ÷, /	• Make predictions about how data will change in the future • Convert from one unit of measurement to another • Find the areas and volumes of objects
Writing Equations	=	• Show that two values are equal
Stating Inequalities	>, <	• Compare the sizes of numbers or objects

Remember that addition and subtraction are inverse, or opposite, operations. So are multiplication and division. Using one operation undoes the effect of its opposite. That is why adding 2 and 2 gives you 4, and subtracting 2 from 4 takes you back to 2. Similarly, multiplying 2 and 3 gives you 6, and dividing 6 by 3 takes you back to 2.

A scientist is studying plants. The scientist wants to know how many plants of different kinds there are in a garden. The math operation that would be most useful for the scientist is

A adding

B subtracting

C multiplying

D dividing

This scientist is counting the number of plants in the garden. Adding is the skill you use when you count objects. Choice A is correct.

Using Math in Science

Much of the work that scientists do involves making measurements and collecting data. Scientists use math to help them make sense of the data they collect. Scientists mainly use four math operations: addition, subtraction, multiplication, and division.

Scientists must often count many different kinds of things. They use addition to figure out the total number of things they have counted. For example, a scientist may measure how much rain falls in an area each day for one year. She can add up her measurements to find how much rain fell in the area for the whole year.

The scientist might continue to collect data. After five years, she has collected enough data to make this table:

INCHES OF RAINFALL IN AN AREA

	Year 1	Year 2	Year 3	Year 4	Year 5
Rainfall (in.)	9.0	8.5	7.9	9.2	10.0

To find the total rainfall the area received during this time, the scientist would add all five numbers together, like this:

$$9.0 + 8.5 + 7.9 + 9.2 + 10.0 = 44.6$$

The area received 44.6 inches of rain during these five years.

The scientist wants to determine the difference between the amount of rain that fell in year 1 and the amount of rain that fell in year 5. Explain which math skill the scientist should use, and then solve the problem.

To find the difference between two measurements, use subtraction. The scientist should subtract the amount of rain that fell in year 1 (9.0 inches) from the amount of rain that fell in year 5 (10.0 inches): 10.0 inches − 9.0 inches = 1.0 inch. In year 5, 1.0 inch more rain fell than in year 1.

Suppose the scientist wants to know the average amount of rain that fell each year. To find the average, she can use division. She can divide the total amount of rain by the number of years she measured the rain. She measured the rain for five years. So, she could find the average this way:

$$\frac{44.6 \text{ inches}}{5 \text{ years}} = 8.92 \text{ inches per year}$$

To find an average, add the values in a data set. Then divide the sum of the values by the number of values.

Using Equations and Inequalities

Scientists use an **equation** to show when two values are the same. For example, they can write an equation like the one below:

5 cups × 20 mL of water in each cup = 100 mL of water

This equation could help a scientist find how much water she needs for an experiment. The equals sign shows that the value on the left is the same as the value on the right.

Scientists can write an **inequality** to show when two values are *not* the same. The symbol > means "is greater than." The symbol < means "is less than." For example, 9 < 10 means "9 is less than 10," and 9 > 8 means "9 is greater than 8." Take another look at the data table from the previous page:

INCHES OF RAINFALL IN AN AREA

	Year 1	Year 2	Year 3	Year 4	Year 5
Rainfall (in.)	9.0	8.5	7.9	9.2	10.0

We can use inequalities to compare the amounts of rainfall the area received in different years. For example, we can write this inequality:

rainfall in year 1 > rainfall in year 2
because 9.0 > 8.5

This tells us that the rainfall in year 1 was greater than the rainfall in year 2. We can also write this inequality:

rainfall in year 3 < rainfall in year 4

This tells us that the rainfall in year 3 was less than the rainfall in year 4.

A student measures the masses of three rock samples. Sample 1 has a mass of 53.8 grams. Sample 2 has a mass of 58.9 grams. Sample 3 has a mass of 54.1 grams. Which of these inequalities is true?

A mass of sample 1 > mass of sample 2

B mass of sample 2 < mass of sample 3

C mass of sample 3 < mass of sample 1

D mass of sample 3 < mass of sample 2

The mass of sample 3 is less than the mass of sample 2, because 54.1 < 58.9. Therefore, choice D is correct.

An **equation** is a mathematical statement that uses an equals sign (=) to show that two values are equal.

An **inequality** is a mathematical statement that uses an inequality sign (>, <) to show that one value is greater than or less than another value.

In an inequality, the symbol *always* points toward the smaller number. For example, in the inequality 1 < 2, the < sign points to the 1 because 1 is smaller than 2.

It's Your Turn

Please read each question carefully. For each multiple-choice question, circle the letter of the correct response.

1 **A scientist wants to know how different soils affect tomato plants. She separates 48 plants into 6 equal-sized groups. She tests 1 soil on each group. What operation should she use to find how many plants are in each group?**

A multiplication

B division

C addition

D subtraction

2 **A mallard duck lays 8 eggs. If one-quarter of the eggs do not hatch, how many of the eggs hatch?**

A 2

B 4

C 6

D 8

Base your answers to questions 3 and 4 on the information below.

Each day at noon for one week, a student measures the temperature outside his classroom. He records the data in the following table:

NOONTIME TEMPERATURE OUTSIDE A CLASSROOM

	Monday	Tuesday	Wednesday	Thursday	Friday
Temperature (°C)	28	27	31	29	30

3 **How much did the noontime temperature increase between Tuesday and Wednesday?**

A 3°C

B 4°C

C 27°C

D 31°C

For this open-ended question, write your answer on the line.

4 **Write an inequality to compare the temperature on Monday to the temperature on Wednesday.**

_____

Collecting and Displaying Data

Major Understandings 1M3.1a; 1S2.3a, b; 1S3.1a; 4PS3.1d; 6KI2.3; 6KI5.1

Remember that scientists use data to answer questions. Some data are numbers. For example, data about a leaf might be that it is 5 cm long and 2 cm wide. Most data that are numbers come from measurements.

Some data are not numbers. They are words, pictures, or other descriptions. For example, some data about the leaf might be that it is green, has rough edges, and feels fuzzy. Scientists can use both kinds of data (numbers and words) to draw conclusions.

Tools for Collecting Data

Scientists collect many kinds of data using only their senses. For example, a scientist may look closely at a plant to learn the color and shape of its leaves.

Scientists also use **tools** to collect data. Tools help scientists collect data more clearly. For example, a scientist may use a video camera to record what something looks and sounds like. Tools can also help scientists make exact measurements. For example, a scientist cannot use her senses to say exactly how tall a plant is. She could use a ruler to measure exactly how tall the plant is.

Scientists use different tools for different purposes. Some tools help them see things. Others help them measure things. The pictures below show some common science tools and what you can use them for.

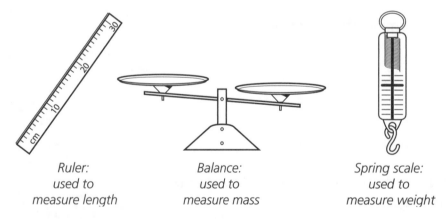

Ruler:
used to
measure length

Balance:
used to
measure mass

Spring scale:
used to
measure weight

You can use a ruler to measure length. You can use a balance to measure **mass** and a spring scale to measure **weight.**

Scientists use **tools** to take measurements or collect data.

Mass is the amount of matter in an object. The mass of an object is the same no matter where it is in the universe.

Weight is the pull of gravity acting on an object. The weight of an object depends on how close it is to other objects, such as Earth.

Mass and weight are related. The more mass an object has, the heavier it is. But mass and weight are not the same. For example, you would have the same mass on the Moon and on Earth. However, you would weigh less on the Moon than you do on Earth. That's because the Moon's gravity is weaker than Earth's gravity.

Thermometer: used to measure temperature

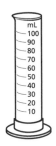

Graduated cylinder: used to measure the volume of a liquid

Graph paper: used to organize data

You can use a thermometer to measure **temperature.** You can use a **graduated cylinder** to measure the **volume** of a liquid. You can use graph paper to organize your data into graphs or charts.

What tool should you use to measure the mass of an acorn?

A balance

B ruler

C stopwatch

D thermometer

A ruler measures length, so choice B is incorrect. A stopwatch measures time, so choice C is incorrect. A thermometer measures temperature, so choice D is incorrect. A balance measures mass, so choice A is the correct answer.

When you make measurements, you should be sure to write them down correctly. You should also record the units of your measurements.

Scientists use abbreviations when they record data. They do not write out full sentences. For example, suppose you measure the height of a friend. You find that he is 120 centimeters tall. You could record this in your journal by writing *height of friend: 120 cm.*

Scientists commonly use metric units of measurement. The table on the next page shows some metric units and their abbreviations. The table also shows some nonmetric units that people use in everyday life.

Temperature is how hot or cold something is.

A **graduated cylinder** is a tall, thin container with markings on it that allows you to measure how much liquid is in it.

Volume is how much space something takes up.

EXAMPLES OF UNITS AND ABBREVIATIONS

Measurement	Metric Units	Nonmetric Units
Length	kilometers (km) meters (m) centimeters (cm) millimeters (mm)	miles (mi) yards (yd) feet (ft) inches (in.)
Mass	kilograms (kg) grams (g) milligrams (mg)	none common
Weight	newtons (N)	pounds (lb) ounces (oz)
Volume	liters (L) milliliters (mL)	gallons (gal) quarts (qt) cups (c)
Temperature	degrees Celsius (°C)	degrees Fahrenheit (°F)
Time	hours (hr) minutes (min) seconds (s)	

Scientists usually use metric units to describe measurements. However, sometimes scientists use nonmetric units. For example, *meteorologists* (scientists who study the weather) commonly describe the amount of rainfall in inches instead of centimeters.

Look at the picture of the toy car below.

Identify the tool you should use to measure the length of the car. Measure the length of the car in the picture. Record the length of the car in centimeters in the space below.

You should use a ruler to measure the length of the car. To use a ruler, hold it so that the "0" end is lined up with the end of the car. Read the number on the ruler that is lined up with the other end of the car. The picture below shows how to do this.

The mark on the ruler that is closest to the right end of the toy car is the 6-cm mark. Therefore, this car is 6 cm long.

Using Tables to Record Data

Scientists often display their data in data tables. **Data tables** show the actual data a scientist has collected. Most data tables show

A **data table** is a model that presents data in columns and rows.

numbers or short descriptions. They do not usually show pictures or drawings.

A data table contains rows and columns. Rows are horizontal. Columns are vertical. In many data tables, each row represents a set of measurements. Each column represents a different kind of measurement. Let's look at an example of how to use a data table to show data.

Casey's class is studying weather. They collected data every day for five days. They measured the temperature at noon. They also observed the weather conditions at their school. They wrote the data in their journals. To organize the data, the class can make a data table like this one:

WEATHER FOR FIVE DAYS

Date	Temperature at Noon (°C)	Weather Conditions
September 5	27	cloudy
September 6	22	rainy
September 7	25	cloudy
September 8	25	cloudy
September 9	28	sunny

Using Graphs to Present Data

Scientists often use graphs to present their data. A graph can help scientists see patterns in the data. Different kinds of graphs are useful for different kinds of data. They may also show the same data in different ways. A graph should have labels and a title that tell you what information the graph contains.

You can use a **bar graph** to compare the sizes of groups or measurements. In a bar graph, each bar represents a different group or measurement. The height of each bar represents the size of the group. Casey and his classmates could use a bar graph to compare the numbers of cloudy, rainy, and sunny days. Their graph would look like the one below.

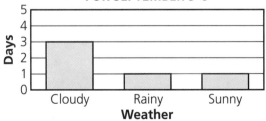

NUMBER OF CLOUDY, RAINY, AND SUNNY DAYS FOR SEPTEMBER 5–9

This bar graph helps you see easily that the week had more cloudy days than rainy or sunny days.

A data table should have a title. The title should tell you what kind of information is in the table. A good title helps others understand the data. The title sums up the data that are in the table.

Graphs can make patterns in data easier to see.

A **bar graph** is a graph that shows the sizes of different groups or objects using different-sized bars.

Please read each question carefully. For each multiple-choice question, circle the letter of the correct response.

1 **A scientist wants to collect data to find out which container best keeps ice from melting. He puts three ice cubes in three separate containers and waits five minutes. What should the scientist measure after the five minutes have passed?**

A the amount of water in each container using a graduated cylinder

B the length of each container using a ruler

C the weight of the ice and water in each container using a spring scale

D the mass of each container using a balance

2 **A student is studying the sizes of different kinds of apples. She uses a spring scale to measure the weights of the apples. The picture shows one of the apples she measures.**

What is the weight of the apple?

A 3.5 N

B 4.0 N

C 4.5 N

D 5.0 N

3 Which of the following units could a student use to describe the length of a snail shell?

A kilograms or ounces

B centimeters or inches

C newtons or pounds

D seconds or minutes

4 A student did an experiment to find out if daisy plants need sunlight to produce flowers. She put plants in four different places with different amounts of sunlight. After six weeks, she counted the total number of flowers on the plants in each place. The table shows her data.

NUMBER OF FLOWERS ON PLANTS IN DIFFERENT LIGHT CONDITIONS

Amount of Light	Number of Flowers After Six Weeks
Full Sun	50
Partial Sun	20
Indirect Sun	10
No Sunlight	0

Which of the following graphs best represents the student's data?

A
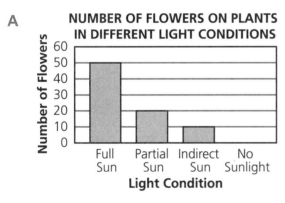

C
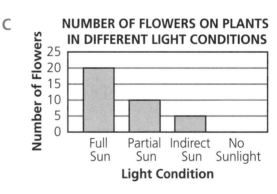

B
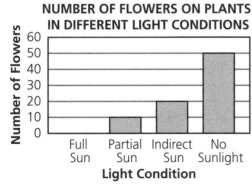

D
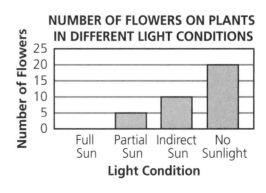

For this open-ended question, write your answers in the table.

5 **A student hangs a cup from a spring. He adds masses to the cup. He measures how far the spring stretches for each mass. He notices that when the mass doubles, the stretch of the spring doubles. Complete the table to show the student's data.**

AMOUNT OF STRETCH OF A SPRING

Mass in Cup	Stretch of Spring
10 g	5 cm
20 g	
40 g	
80 g	

UNIT 1 Analysis, Inquiry, and Design, Part 1

Analyzing Data and Drawing Conclusions

Major Understandings 1M1.1c; 1M2.1a, b; 1S3.2a; 1S3.4a, b; 6KI5.1, 2

Scientists collect data in order to answer scientific questions. Once they have the data, they **analyze** it.

Scientists analyze data to help them draw conclusions. You probably draw conclusions all the time. For example, when you woke up this morning, you may have noticed that it was dark in the room. You may also have heard wind and a tapping sound on the roof. You analyzed these clues, or observations. Then you may have concluded that it was raining.

When scientists **analyze** data, they look for patterns in the data. They may also look for relationships between things.

A **trend** is a pattern in how the data are related to each other.

Analyzing Data

After a scientist collects data, he or she will analyze the data. To analyze data, a scientist might study a graph of the data. The scientist looks for **trends,** or patterns, in the graph. For example, a scientist studying the average temperature in New York City recorded the following data:

AVERAGE TEMPERATURE IN NEW YORK CITY

Year	Average Temperature (°F)
2003	53.4
2004	54.5
2005	55.8
2006	56.8

To analyze the data, the scientist created the line graph shown below.

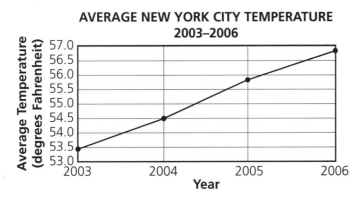

To identify a trend in the data, the scientist can look for a pattern. You can probably see the pattern in these data. Every year has a higher average temperature than the year before. In other words, the average temperature increases every year.

This graph shows how many white-tailed deer lived in a forest as the size of the forest changed.

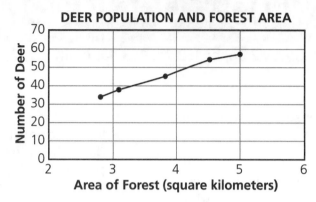

What is the trend shown on the graph?

   A Deer population increases as forest area decreases.

   B Deer population increases as forest area increases.

   C Deer population does not depend on forest area.

   D Deer population and forest area both increase over time.

The graph does not give you any information about time, so choice D is incorrect. When the area of the forest is about 3 square kilometers, about 35 deer live there. When the area of the forest is about 5 square kilometers, about 60 deer live there. Therefore, deer population depends on the size of the forest, so choice C is incorrect. More deer live in the forest when the forest is larger. Therefore, choice A is incorrect. The correct answer is B.

Drawing a Conclusion

When you analyze data, you often have to make **inferences.** An inference is a guess based on data. It is not something you observe directly. For example, suppose your friend comes to school with wet hair and clothes. Wet hair and clothes are clues, or observations. You can combine these observations with your knowledge that your friend walks to school. You can infer that your friend got wet because it is raining outside.

Inferences can be wrong. For example, your friend may be wet because she accidentally walked through a sprinkler. Your inference that it is raining would then be wrong.

Scientists analyze data to draw **conclusions.** A conclusion is an answer to a scientific question. For example, suppose a student does an experiment to study bar magnets. She asks, "What are some characteristics of magnets?" She tests several bar magnets. She observes that every bar magnet she tests can pick up a small piece of metal. She uses this information to draw a conclusion. She

> An **inference** is a guess you make using the data you have.

> A **conclusion** is an answer to a scientific question.

concludes that all magnets can pick up small pieces of metal. This conclusion is an inference. She is making a guess about all magnets, even though she has tested only bar magnets.

You should always use data to support your conclusions. When you draw conclusions, always consider *all* of the data you have.

For example, some rubber balls are hard, but others are not. If you observe both hard and soft rubber balls, you cannot make the conclusion that all rubber balls are hard. You cannot ignore the soft rubber balls just because they do not fit your conclusion.

The table below describes how a student set up an experiment.

CONDITIONS OF AN EXPERIMENT WITH PLANTS

	Group 1	Group 2
Type of plant	green beans	green beans
Location	windowsill	windowsill
Type of water	filtered tap water	rainwater (collected outside)
Amount of water	50 mL per day	50 mL per day
Type of soil	potting soil	potting soil
Amount of sunlight	8.5 hr per day	8.5 hr per day

After three weeks, the student notices that the plants in group 1 are bright green and have many leaves. The plants in group 2 are browner and have fewer leaves. Which of the following is the best conclusion for the student to draw?

A Green beans grow taller in potting soil than in topsoil.

B Green beans need more sun than peas need.

C Green beans grow more leaves when they get filtered water than when they get rainwater.

D Green beans die if they do not get enough water.

The variable in this experiment is the type of water each plant receives. The amount of sunlight, the type of plant, and the type of soil are the same for all the plants. Therefore, choices A and B are incorrect. All of the plants get the same amount of water, so choice D is incorrect. The only difference between the plants is the type of water they get. Therefore, the student can conclude that the rainwater is causing the plants to turn brown. The correct answer is C.

Using Data to Draw Conclusions

A class learned that the water in one part of their town had chemicals in it. The water in another part of town did not. Their teacher told the class that chemicals that spill on soil can move through the soil into the water. The class asked the question "Do chemicals move through all soils at the same speed?" The class did an experiment to try to answer their question.

The class predicted that the chemicals would pass through soils at different speeds. They thought chemicals would pass through sand the fastest.

The class filled clear plastic cups with four different soil materials. They put clay in one cup, dirt in another cup, sand in a third cup, and gravel in a fourth cup. Each cup was the same size. They put holes in the bottom of each cup. All the holes were the same size, and they put the same number of holes in each cup.

The class decided to use apple juice to represent chemicals. They poured the same amount of apple juice onto the material in each cup. They measured how long it took for the juice to drip from the holes in the bottom of the cup.

Then, the class looked at the pieces in each kind of material. They observed how large the pieces in each material were. The table shows what they recorded.

FLOW RATE OF APPLE JUICE IN DIFFERENT SOIL MATERIALS

Material in Cup	Size of Pieces	Time for Juice to Drip Out
Clay	very small	juice did not come out
Dirt	small	15 seconds
Sand	medium	4 seconds
Gravel	large	1 second

What can the class conclude about the relationship between soil particle size and the time it takes chemicals to pass through the soil? Use evidence to support your answer.

They can conclude that chemicals pass through soil with small particles more slowly than they pass through soil with larger particles. Clay has a very small particle size, and it took 30 seconds for the chemicals to pass through it. Dirt has a larger particle size, and it took less time (15 seconds) for chemicals to pass through. This trend continued for sand and gravel.

Notice that the results of the class's experiment did not fully support their prediction. They predicted that the apple juice would flow through sand the fastest. However, the apple juice flowed through gravel the fastest.

Asking New Questions

Scientists do not stop investigating once they have drawn a conclusion. In many cases, their data make them think of new questions to test. Then, they carry out new investigations to answer their new questions.

The data from this experiment make the class think of another question to test. Which of the following is most likely the question the class thinks of?

   A How well do plants grow in different kinds of soil?

   B How does pollution in drinking water make people sick?

   C How does mixing different kinds of soil materials affect the flow rate of apple juice?

   D How many kinds of sand particles are there?

All of the questions are scientific questions. You need to decide which question the class would *most likely* ask after they studied the data from the experiment. The new question is probably related to the question from the first experiment. The experiment did not involve plants or actual pollution, so choices A and B are incorrect. The class studied more than just sand, so choice D is incorrect. It makes sense that the class would wonder whether mixing different kinds of soil materials would affect the results. So, the correct answer is C.

The results of an experiment can make a scientist ask questions that he or she had not thought about before. Even results that do not agree with a scientist's predictions can be useful. They can make the scientist think of new questions to test.

It's Your Turn

Please read each question carefully. For each multiple-choice question, circle the letter of the correct response.

Base your answers to questions 1 and 2 on the information below.

A student does an investigation to study magnets. She asks, "How is the length of a magnet related to its strength?" She predicts that longer magnets will be stronger than shorter magnets. She tests five different magnets. She tests each magnet by observing how many paper clips it can pick up. The table below shows the data she collects.

STRENGTH OF MAGNETS

Size of Magnet	Number of Paper Clips Picked Up
very short	1
short	5
medium	8
long	4
very long	6

1 Based on the data, the student's prediction was

A   completely correct

B   partly correct; some long magnets are weaker than some short magnets

C   partly correct; the shortest magnets are the strongest

D   completely incorrect

2 The student asks a new question based on her observations. Which of the following questions does she most likely ask?

A   What kinds of metals can magnets pick up?

B   How much heavier are large paper clips than small paper clips?

C   How is the mass of a magnet related to the strength of the magnet?

D   Which magnets stick together most strongly?

Base your answers to questions 3 and 4 on the information below and your knowledge of science.

A scientist did an experiment to identify an unknown chemical. She mixed the chemical into a container of water. She knows that if the temperature of the water increases, the unknown chemical is chemical A. If the temperature of the water decreases, the unknown chemical is chemical B. She measured the temperature of the water every minute. The graph shows her results.

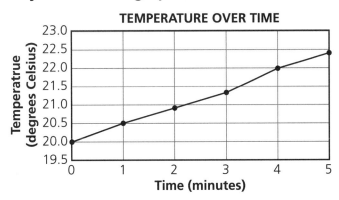

TEMPERATURE OVER TIME

3 The temperature of the water

A   does not change over time

B   decreases over time

C   increases over time

D   increases and then decreases over time

4 The data show that the unknown chemical is most likely

A   chemical A

B   chemical B

C   a mixture of chemical A and chemical B

D   neither chemical A nor chemical B

Base your answers to questions 5 and 6 on the information below.

The table shows the heights of four students. It also shows the lengths of the steps they take.

**HEIGHTS AND STEP LENGTHS
OF FOUR STUDENTS**

Student	Height (cm)	Step Length (cm)
A	123	49
B	132	53
C	127	50
D	117	47

5 A person is 175 cm tall. His step length is probably

A 30 cm

B 40 cm

C 70 cm

D 200 cm

For this open-ended question, write your answers on the lines.

6 How is a person's step length related to his or her height? Explain how the data in the table support your conclusion.

_____

_____

_____

UNIT 1 Analysis, Inquiry, and Design, Part 1

Sharing Scientific Ideas

Major Understandings 1S1.2a; 1S2.2a; 1S3.3a

Many people think scientists work alone in laboratories. But working together and sharing ideas is an important part of science.

Working Together

Sharing data is very important in science. Other scientists can help you find mistakes and figure out if you forgot anything.

A group of students counts the different kinds of trees that grow on school grounds. First, each student takes his or her own count. All the students count the same trees. Then, they make the table below.

KINDS OF TREES AT SCHOOL

	Oak	Maple	Beech	Pine
Michael	5	3	7	1
Jessie	4	3	7	2
Koushiki	5	2	7	2
Angel	5	3	6	2

Each student counted 16 trees. However, each student placed at least one tree in a different category than the others did. For each tree, three students had one count and one student had a different count. They all counted the same trees, so there must be mistakes. Until they find the mistakes, the data in the table are not **reliable.**

Information that is **reliable** can be counted on to be correct.

Michael argues that the group should place each tree in the category that received the most votes. Why is this not a good solution to the problem?

One student might know more about trees than the other students. This student would be a more reliable source, even if the other three students disagree. Scientists must support their conclusions with reliable evidence.

The students decide to borrow a field guide to trees from their teacher. This time, they work together to count each tree. They use the field guide to settle any disagreements. When they are finished, they revise their data table.

KINDS OF TREES AT SCHOOL

	Oak	Maple	Beech	Pine
Group	4	4	7	2

The new table shows that most of the students correctly counted the beech and pine trees. However, only Jessie correctly counted the oak trees. Each student missed one of the maples. In fact, in their original counts, the students missed an entire tree. The new table shows that there are 17 trees growing at the school. This example shows how working together and checking your data can help you find mistakes.

Being Skeptical

Suppose you were one of the students counting trees. What would you say if another student told you that she had found a tree made of solid gold? Most likely, you would want to see the tree for yourself. You would want more evidence than just hearing about it from someone else.

Scientists do not believe something is true just because a friend tells them about it. Scientists are **skeptical.** They need to see for themselves, or they need to see data that show a statement is correct. Good scientists accept information and ideas only

> When people are **skeptical,** they do not believe or accept an idea without good evidence.

✔ when data support them
✔ when they come from reliable sources
✔ when they make sense

Good scientists do not accept information or ideas just because

✘ they heard them from people they like
✘ the ideas are popular

Mark finds a seed on a farm. He wants to know how to make it grow. Which source will have the best information about the seed?

A a television show on seeds from other countries

B a chapter about seeds in a biology textbook

C a magazine advertisement for a new kind of seed

D an article about farm animals that eat seeds

The television show probably won't focus on the seed Mark found, so choice A is incorrect. Advertisements are not reliable science resources, because they are used to sell things. So, choice C is incorrect. An article about farm animals will not help Mark grow seeds, so choice D is incorrect. Textbooks, encyclopedias, and science magazines are all reliable science resources. So, choice B is correct.

Listening to Others' Ideas

Scientists may think about the same data in different ways. They may not agree about what the data mean. When this happens, scientists share their thoughts with each other. They compare the evidence for each idea. They try to figure out which idea is most likely to be correct.

When you do an investigation, you should share your results with others. Then, they can review your results and draw their own conclusions. Talk to others about your conclusions. If you disagree, talk about why. Think about the evidence for your idea and for their ideas. If more evidence supports their ideas, yours may be wrong.

Scientists can still learn a lot from ideas that are not supported by tests. That is because knowing something does not work can point you toward something that does work.

Jamal dissolves different chemicals in water. He lets the water evaporate. Then, he studies the sizes of the crystals that form. The table shows his setup and results.

CRYSTAL EXPERIMENT SETUP AND RESULTS

Jar	Type of Chemical	Amount of Chemical	Amount of Water	Temperature	Average Size of Crystals
1	sugar	15 g	100 mL	30°C	about 2 mm across
2	sugar	15 g	100 mL	30°C	about 2 mm across
3	sugar	15 g	100 mL	30°C	about 2 mm across
4	salt	15 g	100 mL	20°C	about 4 mm across
5	salt	15 g	100 mL	20°C	about 4 mm across
6	salt	15 g	100 mL	20°C	about 4 mm across

Jamal thinks that salt is made up of larger particles than sugar is, because salt forms larger crystals. He shares his results with Sue. She thinks the salt crystals were larger because they grew at a lower temperature. What is the best way for Jamal to figure out whether Sue is likely to be correct?

A ask their classmates to vote on whose idea they like best

B repeat the experiment in exactly the same way

C repeat the experiment and keep all temperatures the same

D ignore both ideas and look for a third explanation

Popular ideas are not always right, so choice A is incorrect. Repeating the experiment in the same way will give Jamal more data, but will not help him figure out which conclusion is right. Choice B is incorrect. You should never ignore an explanation unless you have a reason to ignore it. Choice D is incorrect. The best way to figure out which idea is correct is to look for evidence to support each idea. An idea that has a lot of evidence supporting it is likely to be correct. Jamal can repeat the experiment with all the temperatures the same. If the crystals are still different sizes, that is evidence that supports his idea. The correct answer is C.

It's Your Turn

Please read each question carefully. For each multiple-choice question, circle the letter of the correct response.

1 **A student wants to do an experiment to learn how mass affects the speed of an object. She plans to test a golf ball, a tennis ball, and a bowling ball. She plans to roll each ball down a ramp. She will then measure how far each ball rolls. She asks her friends for suggestions on how to make her experiment better. Which of these suggestions should she follow?**

    A use balls that all have the same mass but different textures

    B make the height of the ramp different for each ball

    C drop the balls onto the ramp

    D use three bowling balls that have different masses but the same size

Base your answers to questions 2 and 3 on the information below.

Magnets stick to some metals, such as steel and iron. Magnets can also make compass needles move. A student tested four different objects that she thought might be magnets. She tested each object in three different ways and recorded her data in the following table.

MAGNETISM TEST FOR FOUR DIFFERENT OBJECTS

Object	Effect on Steel Cabinet	Effect on Steel Pins	Effect on Compass Needle
A	stuck to cabinet	picked up three pins	made compass needle move
B	did not stick to cabinet	did not pick up any pins	did not make compass needle move
C	stuck to cabinet	made pins move, but did not pick any up	made compass needle move a little
D	stuck to cabinet	picked up one pin	made compass needle move

2 **You tell your friend which of the objects you think are magnets. Your friend disagrees with you. What should you do?**

    A tell your friend he is wrong

    B ask your other friends for their opinions

    C compare the evidence for each of your ideas

    D explain the problem to your parents

For this open-ended question, write your answers on the lines.

3 **Look at the table on page 37. Which objects are most likely magnets? Explain how the data in the table support your conclusion.**

_____

_____

_____

UNIT 1 Analysis, Inquiry, and Design, Part 1

Hands-On Lesson: Measuring

Major Understandings 1M1.1b, c; 1M3.1a; 1S2.3a, b; 6KI5.1

In this activity, you will measure the lengths and masses of different objects. You will also learn two different methods for measuring volume.

Materials

- metric ruler
- 5 blocks of different lengths and masses
- two-pan balance with a set of gram masses
- solid wooden block and solid metal block of equal size
- 100 mL graduated cylinder
- beaker with at least 50 mL of water in it
- metal bolt

Part I: Measuring Length

1 Use the metric ruler to measure the length of the shortest block. Place the block next to the ruler so that one end of the block lines up with the 0 mark on the ruler.

Line up the block with the 0 mark on your ruler.

2 The ruler contains both large and small marks. The large marks stand for centimeters (cm). The small marks stand for millimeters (mm). There are 10 mm in 1 cm. A millimeter is one-tenth of a centimeter. So, you can write 1 mm as 0.1 cm. To measure the length of the block, find the number on the last centimeter mark the block passes. On the picture above, that number is 8.

3 Then, count the number of millimeter marks past that number that the block reaches. Use that number as the decimal. The block shown in the picture above reaches to two small marks past the 8. So, the block is 8.2 cm long.

Do *not* line up the block with the end of the ruler itself. On many rulers, the first mark is located slightly to the right of the end. To make an accurate measurement, you must begin at the first mark.

There are 10 mm in 1 cm, and 100 cm in 1 meter (m). So, there are $10 \times 100 = 1{,}000$ mm in 1 m.

Not every ruler measures length in metric units. The most common *nonstandard* units for measuring length are inches. Be sure to use a metric ruler for this activity.

Question 1: Measure the lengths of the five blocks. Record your measurements in the table below. Give your measurements to the nearest millimeter.

TABLE 1

	Block 1	Block 2	Block 3	Block 4	Block 5
Length to the Nearest Millimeter					

Part II: Measuring Mass

Question 2: Look at the wooden block and the metal block, but do not pick them up. Which do you think has the greater mass? Explain your answer.

_____

_____

_____

1 Place the wooden block on the left-hand pan of the two-pan balance. Note how that pan sinks and the right-hand pan rises. This is because the left-hand pan is supporting more mass than the right-hand pan. To make the two pans level again, you need to add mass to the right-hand pan.

2 Observe the different gram masses that come with the two-pan balance. Each gram mass is labeled with a number followed by the letter *g*. The letter *g* stands for "grams." Grams are the standard metric unit of mass.

3 Place the largest gram mass on the right-hand pan. If the right-hand pan sinks below the level of the left-hand pan, remove the gram mass. Place the next-largest gram mass on the right-hand pan. If the right-hand pan sinks below the left-hand pan, remove this gram mass as well. Continue to test each gram mass until you find a gram mass that does not cause the right-hand pan to sink below the left-hand pan.

4 Add smaller gram masses to the right-hand pan until it sinks to the same level as the left-hand pan, as shown below.

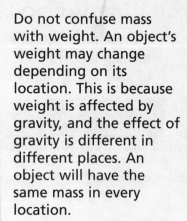

Do not confuse mass with weight. An object's weight may change depending on its location. This is because weight is affected by gravity, and the effect of gravity is different in different places. An object will have the same mass in every location.

There are 1,000 grams in 1 kilogram (kg).

When both pans are at the same level, the scale is balanced.

5 Add up the numbers on the gram masses on the right-hand pan. The total is the mass of the wooden block. For example, in the image on the previous page, the wooden block has a mass of 5 g + 1 g + 1 g = 7 g.

Question 3: What is the mass of the wooden block?

_____

6 Repeat steps 2–5 for the metal block.

Question 4: What is the mass of the metal block?

_____

Question 5: Was your guess in question 2 correct? Explain your answer.

_____

_____

Part III: Measuring Volume

1 Study the graduated cylinder. Note the marks along the side. These marks are similar to the marks on a ruler. However, the marks on a graduated cylinder measure volume. The metric unit for volume is the milliliter (mL). Each mark on your graduated cylinder stands for 1 mL.

2 Pour water from the beaker into the graduated cylinder until the water level reaches the 50-mL mark. You may notice that the water forms a slight curve inside the cylinder. This curve is called a *meniscus*. To read the volume of the liquid, look at the bottom of the meniscus. If there is no meniscus, read the volume of water from the level of the water's surface.

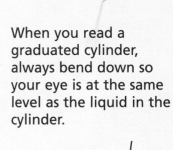

When you read a graduated cylinder, always bend down so your eye is at the same level as the liquid in the cylinder.

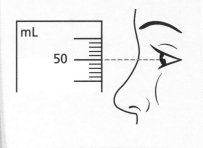

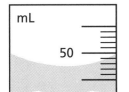 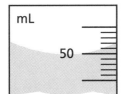 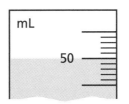

The graduated cylinder on the left contains 48 mL of liquid. The graduated cylinders in the middle and on the right each contain 50 mL of liquid.

Question 6: What is the volume of water in the graduated cylinder? Record your answer to the nearest milliliter.

_____

To find the volume of a liquid, you can pour the liquid into a graduated cylinder and read the mark that lines up with the meniscus. Why can't you use the same process to find the volume of a solid metal bolt?

A metal bolt is a solid. Unlike liquids, solids do not change shape to fill their containers. There will be empty space around the bolt that keeps you from measuring exactly how much space it takes up.

3 Carefully place the bolt in the graduated cylinder. The water level will rise.

Question 7: What is the total volume of the bolt and the water? Record your answer to the nearest milliliter.

_____

Question 8: How can you use this information to find the volume of the bolt?

_____

_____

_____

Question 9: What is the volume of the bolt? Record your answer to the nearest milliliter.

_____

Analysis, Inquiry, and Design, Part 1 Review

Please read each question carefully. For each multiple-choice question, circle the letter of the correct response.

1 **A student visits a zoo and sees many different animals. She thinks of a scientific question about the animals she sees. Which question does she most likely think of?**

  A   Are spiders uglier than flies?

  B   Do monkeys smell worse than lizards?

  C   Do turtles move faster than snails?

  D   Are swans prettier than doves?

2 **A scientist is studying frogs from different countries. Which of these predictions could she test with a scientific investigation?**

  A   Costa Rican frogs have easier lives than Canadian frogs.

  B   American frogs are happier than Australian frogs.

  C   Australian frogs have better lives than American frogs.

  D   South African frogs live longer than Canadian frogs.

3 **A student wants to investigate the relationship between the mass of a ball and the distance it will roll. He measures the mass of each ball using a balance. Then, he places each ball at the top of a ramp and releases it. What is the best step for the student to do next?**

  A   Measure how far each ball rolls.

  B   Record the mass of each ball.

  C   Repeat the experiment.

  D   Graph the results.

4 A scientist is studying bacteria. He knows that the number of bacteria doubles every 2 hours. He wants to know how many bacteria there will be after a month. Which math operation would be most useful for the scientist?

A adding

B subtracting

C multiplying

D dividing

5 A student does an experiment to see if the temperature in a room affects plant growth. Which tool should she use to collect temperature data?

A

C

B

D

Base your answers to questions 6 and 7 on the table below and on your knowledge of science.

A scientist is testing the effects of different fuels on race cars. She tests three identical race cars. She uses a different fuel in each car and then races the cars on the same track. The table shows the results.

RACE CAR FINISHING TIMES

Car	Type of Fuel	Finishing Time
A	fuel 1	3 minutes, 40 seconds
B	fuel 2	2 minutes, 55 seconds
C	fuel 3	3 minutes, 45 seconds

6 Based on this information, which of the following is true?

A   time of car A $<$ time of car B

B   time of car A $<$ time of car C

C   time of car B $>$ time of car C

D   time of car C $=$ time of car A

7 The scientist thinks fuel 2 makes the cars travel fastest because it contains more energy. Which of these observations would most likely make the scientist change her explanation?

A   Car A travels faster when it uses fuel 2.

B   Car C travels slower when it uses fuel 2.

C   Car B travels slower when it uses fuel 3.

D   Car A travels slower when it uses fuel 1.

8 A student shined light of three different colors on three radish plants. He measured how tall they grew after two weeks. The plant that got red light grew 15 cm. The plant that got green light grew 8 cm. The plant that got blue light grew 14 cm. Which table best represents these data?

A   HEIGHTS OF PLANTS GROWN UNDER DIFFERENT COLORS OF LIGHT

Color of light	red	15 cm
Color of light	green	8 cm
Color of light	green	14 cm

C   HEIGHTS OF PLANTS GROWN UNDER DIFFERENT COLORS OF LIGHT

Plant	1	2	3
Color of light	red	red	red
Color of light	green	green	green
Color of light	blue	blue	blue
Height after 2 weeks	15 cm	8 cm	14 cm

B   HEIGHTS OF PLANTS GROWN UNDER DIFFERENT COLORS OF LIGHT

Height after 2 weeks	15 cm	14 cm	8 cm
Color of light	red	green	blue

D   HEIGHTS OF PLANTS GROWN UNDER DIFFERENT COLORS OF LIGHT

Plant	Color of light	Height after 2 weeks
1	red	15 cm
2	green	8 cm
3	blue	14 cm

9 A student wants to report the distance from his house to school in both metric and nonmetric units. Which two units could he use?

A   liters and ounces

B   kilograms and pounds

C   kilometers and miles

D   degrees Celsius and degrees Fahrenheit

10 A student measures the length of an insect. It is 14.6 cm long. What is the best way for the student to record the measurement in her journal?

A   insect: 14

B   length of insect: 14.6 cm

C   14.6 cm

D   insect: about 14 cm

11 What is the height of the plant shown below?

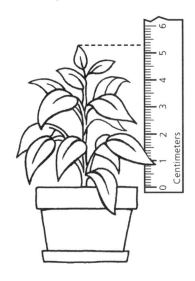

- **A**   5 mm
- **B**   3 cm
- **C**   5.3 cm
- **D**   53 cm

12 Adult frogs lay eggs. The eggs hatch into tadpoles. The tadpoles grow into adults. Which of these models best represents the life cycle of frogs?

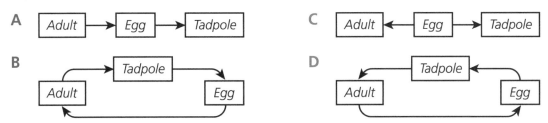

13 A student wants to see if there is a relationship between a person's height and the size of his or her feet. The best way for him to collect data would be to

- **A**   ask people if they have large feet
- **B**   weigh each person using a spring scale
- **C**   measure the lengths of people's feet using a ruler
- **D**   record each person's age on graph paper

14 When a scientist did an experiment studying the populations of different types of fish, he noticed that many tuna fish were swimming south. What new question would the scientist most likely ask?

A Where are the tuna fish swimming to?

B Do trout prefer warmer or cooler water?

C How many different types of fish are there?

D What is the population of salmon in Iceland?

Base your answers to questions 15 and 16 on the table below and on your knowledge of science.

A scientist is studying birds. He observes the birds in a small park for four weeks. The table shows his observations.

OBSERVATIONS OF BIRDS IN A LOCAL PARK

Type of Bird	Average Number Seen Per Day
blue jay	10
robin	6
chickadee	15
goldfinch	4

15 Which of these statements is most likely true?

A More blue jays than chickadees live in the park.

B More robins than goldfinches live in the park.

C More robins than blue jays live in the park.

D More goldfinches than chickadees live in the park.

16 The scientist concludes that the park contains more food that chickadees eat than food that goldfinches eat. The scientist most likely drew this conclusion because

A he saw many more blue jays than goldfinches

B he saw more robins than goldfinches

C he saw more chickadees than blue jays

D he saw many more chickadees than goldfinches

Base your answers to questions 17 and 18 on the table below and on your knowledge of science.

A student investigated how two kinds of mold grew on two different kinds of food. She used four different plates. Two of the plates had applesauce on them. The other two had vanilla pudding on them. She put some of each kind of mold on each of the different kinds of food. She used the same amount of mold on each plate. The table below shows the kinds of mold and kinds of food on each plate.

KINDS OF MOLD AND KINDS OF FOOD ON FOUR PLATES

Plate	Kind of Mold	Kind of Food
1	A	applesauce
2	A	vanilla pudding
3	B	applesauce
4	B	vanilla pudding

After one week, the student observed the plates to see how the mold had grown. The pictures below show what she saw.

Plate 1: Mold A on applesauce *Plate 2: Mold A on vanilla pudding* *Plate 3: Mold B on applesauce* *Plate 4: Mold B on vanilla pudding*

17 The student read a science magazine article about molds. Which of these statements from the article best explains her results?

A "All kinds of mold need food to grow."

B "Some kinds of mold grow best on bread."

C "Many kinds of mold can grow only in dark places."

D "Different kinds of mold grow best on different kinds of food."

18 The student showed her results to four friends. She explained that she wants to learn more about how different molds grow. Each friend suggests a way that she could modify her experiment. Which suggestion would result in a fair experiment?

A Put a different amount of mold on each plate.

B Grow molds A and B on two more kinds of food.

C Grow the mold on each plate at a different temperature.

D Grow a new kind of mold on a plate of strawberries.

19 **A student did an experiment to learn what kind of food attracts the most squirrels. After the student draws his conclusions, he should**

   A   keep his results secret

   B   ignore others' ideas unless they agree with his conclusions

   C   share his conclusions with others and ask whether they agree

   D   ask his friends to vote on whether his ideas are good

For each open-ended question, write your answers on the lines.

20 **The picture below shows the grasshoppers in a garden on two different days.**

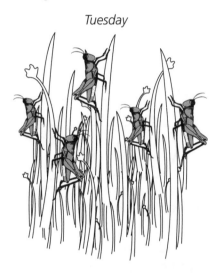
Tuesday

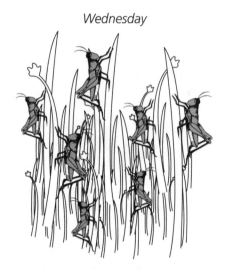
Wednesday

Describe how the number of grasshoppers changed from Tuesday to Wednesday.

_____

_____

21 **A student counted the number of ants walking past her. Eleven ants walked past the student every minute. How many ants walked past her in 20 minutes?**

_____ ants

UNIT 1 Analysis, Inquiry, and Design, Part 1

22 The graph shows the mass of a giant panda during the first year of its life.

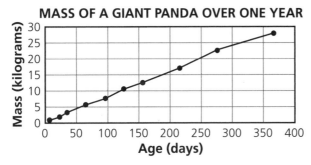

MASS OF A GIANT PANDA OVER ONE YEAR

What pattern is there in the data?

_____

_____

23 A student did an experiment to learn how air temperature affects the size of a balloon. The table shows his results.

DIAMETER OF A BALLOON IN
DIFFERENT TEMPERATURE LOCATIONS

Location	Temperature	Diameter of balloon
In the freezer	–15°C	5 cm
Outside	10°C	8 cm
In the living room	25°C	12 cm

What is the relationship between air temperature and balloon diameter?

_____

_____

Unit 2
Analysis, Inquiry, and Design, Part 2

Systems, models, and patterns help scientists understand and describe the world. They also help engineers design better objects. In this unit, you will learn about systems, models, and patterns. You will also practice science skills, such as making predictions.

There are five lessons in this unit:

1 Systems and Their Parts   Almost everything scientists study is a system. Systems are made up of parts that work together. The parts of a system can be many different sizes. In this lesson, you will learn about different kinds of systems. You will also learn how the parts of a system affect one another.

2 Models   Models represent real objects. They can also represent events or ideas. Scientists use models to help them study the world. In this lesson, you will learn about different kinds of models. You will also learn how to choose the best model for what you want to represent.

3 Change and Patterns   Natural and human-made things change in many ways. Some changes make patterns that repeat over time. Scientists study these patterns to learn more about the world. In this lesson, you will learn how scientists study changes. You will also learn to use patterns to make predictions.

4 Engineering and Design   Engineers design objects for people to use. Sometimes, they change objects to make them safer or more useful. In this lesson, you will learn how engineers solve problems. You will also learn how engineers design objects.

5 Hands-On Lesson: Predicting   Scientists often make predictions. They do investigations to test their predictions. They may make new predictions based on their results. In this lesson, you will create a simple pendulum. You will record data about how it moves. You will then predict how changing its length will affect its motion.

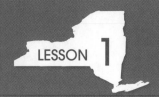

Systems and Their Parts

Major Understandings 6KI1.1, 2; 6KI3.1, 2

Many of the things scientists study are systems. A **system** is a group of parts that work together and affect one another. Everything on Earth is part of one or more systems.

Systems and Their Parts

All systems are made up of parts that interact, or work together. Each part has a different **role,** or job. If one of the roles is not filled, or if something keeps the parts from interacting, the system may not work.

A ballpoint pen is a system. One of the parts is a tiny ball in the tip of the pen. Another part holds the ink inside the pen. The ball rolls around in the tip when someone writes with the pen. As the ball rolls, it gets covered with ink. The ball spreads the ink evenly on the paper. If the ball gets stuck and cannot move, it cannot spread the ink. The pen will not work.

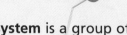

A **system** is a group of parts that work together.

A part's **role** in a system is the job the part does in the system.

The picture below shows a system.

Which of these best describes how parts 1 and 2 interact?

A Watching part 1 makes buttons on part 2 move.

B Turning on part 1 makes part 2 light up.

C Plugging part 2 into part 1 makes part 1 work.

D Typing on part 2 makes symbols appear on part 1.

The picture shows a laptop. Part 1 is the screen. Part 2 is the keyboard. People use the keyboard to type their thoughts into the system. The thoughts appear on the screen as letters and other symbols. Choice D is correct.

A system may be made up of many smaller systems. The keyboard, the screen, and the other parts of a computer are all systems. The computer may be part of an even larger system: the Internet.

Systems and their parts can be very large, very small, or anywhere in between. This is true whether they are natural or human-made. However, nearly all objects have limits on their size. Computers have gotten much smaller since they were invented. But if they become too small, people could no longer use them.

People are limited in size, too. Some are very tall, and others are very short. But people can only grow as tall as their bones and organs allow them to grow. At some point, they simply will not grow any more.

The tallest building in the world is about 800 m tall. Identify <u>two</u> things that limit the sizes of buildings.

> Buildings are limited by the strength of their parts. If they are too tall, they may fall down. Buildings are also limited by the strength of the land beneath them. If they are too big, the land won't support them.

Systems and their parts may be different in other ways, too. They may be different in age. For example, Earth is a system that has existed for billions of years. Other things, such as a baby or a brand-new car, are very young. Systems may also be different in size. Compared to the baby, the car is very large. Compared to Earth, the car is very small.

Examples of Natural Systems

Earth is made up of many different natural systems. Living things, rivers, mountains, oceans, and even Earth itself are all examples of natural systems. The parts of a natural system can be living or nonliving. The parts in a natural system are not human-made.

A forest is an example of a natural system called an ecosystem. An **ecosystem** is all the living and nonliving things in an area. Plants, animals, and other living things are living parts of a forest ecosystem. Rocks, soil, water, and air are nonliving parts of a forest ecosystem. There are many different kinds of ecosystems.

Each part of an ecosystem depends on the other parts. For example, think of the soil in a forest. Many organisms depend on soil. Some animals live in the soil or get their food there. Plants get water and some nutrients from the soil. However, the soil depends

Earth's mass is about six million billion billion kilograms. In contrast, a tiny germ—the kind that might cause you to miss a week of school with a terrible cold—has a mass of less than one-billionth of one gram.

An **ecosystem** is a system made up of all the living and nonliving things in an area.

on organisms, too. Plant roots hold the soil in place when it rains. Nutrients from dead organisms go back into the soil and help other living things grow.

Examples of Human-Made Systems

Most of the things we use every day are human-made systems. Human-made systems include bicycles, computers, maps, the Internet, electric lights, and water pipes. Most human-made systems are made up of nonliving, human-made parts. The pictures below show the parts of two human-made systems.

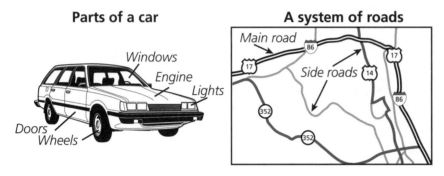

Parts of a car

Windows
Engine
Lights
Doors
Wheels

A system of roads

Main road
Side roads

Which of these systems is most likely made up of nonliving, human-made parts?

   A a mountain

   B a telephone

   C a spider's web

   D a long river

All the systems contain nonliving parts. However, a mountain, a spider's web, and a river are all natural systems. Therefore, they are made up of natural parts. Choices A, C, and D are incorrect. A telephone is a human-made system. It contains human-made parts, such as metal wires and plastic buttons. Choice B is correct.

Not all human-made systems are made up of parts you can touch. Some human-made systems are made up of ideas. Many of these systems are important in science. Scientists develop these systems as they learn more about how the world works. Systems of ideas help scientists understand how different parts of the world are related.

UNIT 2 Analysis, Inquiry, and Design, Part 2

It's Your Turn

Please read each question carefully. For each multiple-choice question, circle the letter of the correct response.

1 **Which of these is the best example of parts of a natural system?**

   A a flower and a rock   **C** a truck and a factory

   B a wire and a battery   **D** a person and a jacket

2 **Which of the objects in these pairs has the <u>largest</u> difference in size?**

   A a bicycle and a car   **C** a pebble and a planet

   B a soccer ball and a baseball   **D** a dog and a puppy

For each open-ended question, write your answers on the lines.

Base your answers to questions 3 and 4 on the picture below.

A scientist is studying a lizard. The picture shows the system she made for the lizard to live in.

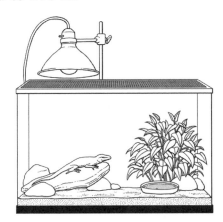

3 **Describe <u>two</u> ways the living and nonliving parts of this system may interact with each other.**

   (1) _____

   (2) _____

4 **Identify <u>two</u> things that limit how big the lizard can grow.**

   (1) _____

   (2) _____

Models

Major Understandings 6KI2.1–3

You have probably seen and used models many times without realizing it. When you find a place on a map or globe, you are using a model. When you draw a picture of something you saw, you are making a model.

What Is a Model?

A **model** is anything that represents an object, an event, or an idea. Globes, maps, and graphs are models. A globe represents a planet such as Earth. A map represents a particular place. A graph represents data.

Scientists make and use models to study the natural world. Many models in science represent objects that are too small, too large, too far away, or too difficult to study directly. Models help scientists learn more about objects in the real world.

There is always some difference between a model and the thing it represents. For example, if you wanted to learn about the planets, you could study a model of the solar system like this one:

> A **model** is something that represents an object, an event, or an idea.

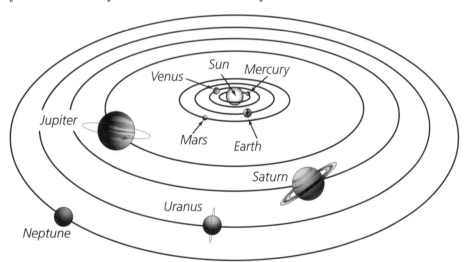

This model of the solar system does not show the real distances of planets from the Sun. However, it does show you the order of the planets.

This model is useful because it shows the locations of the planets. It also shows the paths of the planets as they travel around the Sun. However, the model is different from the actual solar system in many ways. For example, the real planets are much larger than the planets in this model.

Describe <u>one</u> way a globe is similar to Earth and <u>one</u> way a globe is <u>different</u> from Earth.

> A globe is the same shape as Earth. However, a globe is much smaller than Earth.

Types of Models

A map is a common type of model. Some maps show the cities or roads in an area. Other maps show physical characteristics such as mountains, lakes, and rivers.

Other types of models include graphs, sketches, and diagrams. A sketch is a quick drawing of something. Scientists may use sketches to record their observations. Most sketches show only a few parts of an object. Only the parts the scientist is studying are included in the sketch.

A diagram is a labeled picture. A diagram of an ant's body may show a drawing of an ant with different parts labeled. A scientist could study the diagram to learn more about the structure of an ant. Most diagrams show more details than most sketches.

> No single model can show you everything. To study one object or event, you might need to use several different kinds of models.

Making and Using Models

A class wants to study human lungs. They cannot observe lungs directly. So, they decide to make a model of the lungs. They use a plastic soda bottle, a piece of plastic tube, some balloons, a thin piece of rubber, and some clay to make the model. The diagram below shows how they put the model together.

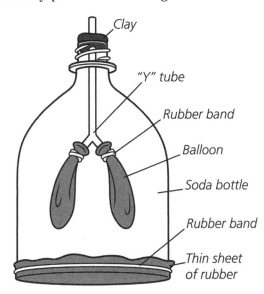

Clay
"Y" tube
Rubber band
Balloon
Soda bottle
Rubber band
Thin sheet of rubber

When a student pulls down on the rubber, the balloons expand. When the student pushes up on the rubber, the balloons collapse.

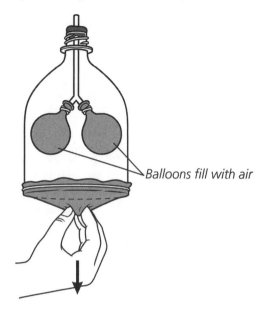

Balloons fill with air

The teacher explains that the thin piece of rubber represents the diaphragm. The diaphragm is a muscle in your body that allows you to breathe. When you inhale, your diaphragm moves down and pulls air into your lungs. This makes your lungs expand. When you exhale, the diaphragm moves up. The air gets pushed back out of your lungs.

The class studies the model to learn more about how the lungs work. Some students have heard that cigarette smoking damages the lungs. They want to understand this better. The teacher explains that cigarette smoking can make the lungs less elastic. This means that they do not stretch as easily.

Based on the model of the lungs, what would most likely happen to a person whose lungs were damaged from cigarette smoke?

   A The person could not swallow easily.

   B The person's throat would burn all the time.

   C The person would run out of breath quickly.

   D The person's heart would beat faster.

> Cigarette smoking makes the lungs less elastic. Think about the balloons in the model. If the balloons did not stretch out as easily, they would not be able to fill up with as much air. Based on the model, a person with damaged lungs would not be able to breathe in much air. This would make the person run out of breath quickly. The correct answer is C.

It's Your Turn

Please read each question carefully. For each multiple-choice question, circle the letter of the correct response.

1 This model shows the Sun and Earth.

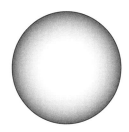 

This model is different from the real Earth-Sun system because it shows

A   that Earth has continents

B   Earth and the Sun very close together

C   that Earth has both day and night

D   Earth smaller than the Sun

2 This model shows the different parts of the water cycle. The arrows show how water moves between the sky, the ground, and the ocean.

Based on this model, what makes water move from the ocean into the sky?

A   groundwater

B   precipitation

C   runoff

D   evaporation

For this open-ended question, write your answer on the line.

3 **A student throws a ball into the air. It lands 10 meters away. She draws the sketch shown below.**

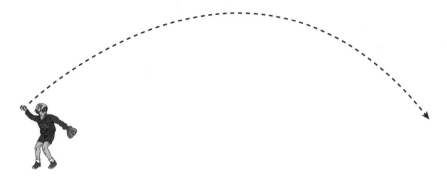

What does the dotted line in the sketch most likely represent?

_____

Change and Patterns

Major Understandings 1M2.1b; 6KI4.1, 2; 6KI5.1, 2

The world around you is always changing. Snow melts on a sunny day. Cars move from place to place. Plants and animals grow over time. Scientists recognize changes in the world by making observations.

Suppose you make observations about a tree. You see that it has green leaves in the summer. You notice that the leaves change from green to yellow in the fall. You also notice that the leaves fall off in the winter and grow back in the spring.

Recognizing and Describing Changes

Scientists analyze the things they observe. They try to figure out what their observations mean. Observing and analyzing the world help scientists recognize when something changes. Observing and analyzing also help them learn what causes the change.

Once scientists recognize a change, they describe it. You can use numbers, words, or pictures to describe changes. You can also describe changes by comparing one object to another. Scientists record their descriptions of changes clearly and carefully.

Change happens when objects move from place to place. You can measure time and distance to describe these changes. Suppose a toy car moved down a ramp. You can measure the time it took for the car to reach the bottom of the ramp. You can also measure the distance the car moved down the ramp. These measurements help you describe how the car's location changed. You can also use these measurements to calculate the car's speed.

If the change is big enough, you can see it with your eyes. However, you must use tools to measure most changes. You can see that the car rolled to the bottom of the ramp. But to know exactly how far it rolled, you need to measure with a ruler. You can also use tools to measure changes that are too small to see with your eyes.

> To find the speed of an object, divide the distance it moved by the time it took to move. You would probably describe the toy car's speed in meters per second (m/s).

The water in a pond changes temperature as the sun shines on it. To best measure this change, you should use

A a ruler

C a thermometer

B your hand

D a magnifying glass

You use a ruler to measure length. You use a magnifying glass to make small objects look bigger. Choices A and D are incorrect. You can feel when temperature changes, but your hand cannot tell you how much the temperature changed. Choice B is incorrect. You can use a thermometer to measure changes in temperature, so the correct answer is C.

Many factors cause things to change. Sunlight helps plants grow. When a plant grows, its height changes. You can measure the height of a plant to describe its growth. You can also describe the change in a plant's height by comparing it to other things. For example, you could say that a plant grew taller than a fence.

Temperature can also cause changes. When you get warm, your body may sweat. Sweating is a way to cool your body. Your body makes this change when temperatures get high. Your body changes in other ways, too. You get taller and heavier as you grow. Your body also changes when you breathe, eat, and use energy.

The field below looks very different in summer than in winter.

Identify <u>one</u> thing that changes in the field between summer and winter. Identify <u>one</u> thing that does not change between summer and winter.

The field changes in many ways between summer and winter. Plants die or lose their leaves, the ground becomes covered in snow, and animals eat different foods. However, some things stay the same. The shape of the land and the types of animals that live there are generally the same from year to year.

Parts of your body are constantly changing in small but important ways. However, your body never changes so much that it stops being your body. This is true of all healthy systems. Different parts may change, but overall the system remains the same.

Food supplies in many environments get smaller in the winter. Some animals do not eat in the winter. They eat extra food in the fall and store it in their bodies as fat. Then they hibernate, or sleep, through the winter and live off the stored fat.

64

UNIT 2 Analysis, Inquiry, and Design, Part 2

Patterns

Remember your observations about the tree. Its green leaves turned yellow in the fall, dropped off in the winter, and grew back in the spring. If you continued to observe this tree, you would see the same pattern each year.

A **pattern** has parts that repeat in a certain order. You might know that numbers and shapes can form patterns. For example, the series of numbers 1, 5, 2, 1, 5, 2, 1, 5, 2, 1, 5, 2 is a pattern. The numbers 1, 5, and 2 repeat in that order within this pattern. Many objects in nature also form patterns. The picture below shows one example.

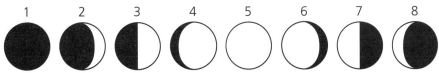

The shapes of the moon repeat in this order every month.

Using Patterns to Make Predictions

Scientists find patterns in the natural world by making observations. Because patterns repeat, scientists use them to make predictions. In other words, they use patterns to guess what will happen in the future.

Suppose a scientist observes leaves growing on a stem. She notices that leaves grow on only one side of the stem. New leaves grow at the top of the stem. Based on this pattern, the scientist can predict that the next leaf will grow on the same side of the stem as the other leaves. It will grow at the top of the stem.

A student observes the time the Sun sets every day during the month of September. He notices that the Sun sets one minute earlier each night. On Monday, the Sun sets at 6:55 P.M. At what time will the Sun most likely set on Wednesday?

A 6:56 P.M.

B 6:55 P.M.

C 6:54 P.M.

D 6:53 P.M.

Each night, the Sun sets one minute earlier. On Monday, the Sun set at 6:55 P.M. Therefore, on Tuesday, the Sun will set one minute earlier, at 6:54 P.M. On Wednesday, the Sun will set one minute earlier than on Tuesday, or 6:53 P.M. Choice D is correct.

Sometimes a pattern can be difficult to see. This is especially true when there are lots of data to analyze. Graphing the data can help you see the pattern. A graph can also help you make predictions about events far in the future.

Suppose you discover a leak in a water barrel. The barrel originally contains 100 liters of water. You observe the barrel throughout the day and record your observations in the table below.

A liter is a metric unit that describes volume. There are 1,000 milliliters in 1 liter.

WATER REMAINING IN A LEAKING BARREL

	0 Hours	1 Hour	5 Hours	10 Hours	24 Hours
Water Left in the Barrel	100 liters	97 liters	85 liters	70 liters	28 liters

You want to know how long it will take for all the water to leak out of the barrel. One solution is to graph the data and look for a pattern.

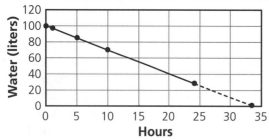

RATE AT WHICH WATER LEAKS FROM A BARREL

The line crosses the bottom of the graph at the point $(33\frac{1}{3}, 0)$. This means that after $33\frac{1}{3}$ hours, there will be 0 liters of water left in the barrel. One-third of an hour is 20 minutes.

The graph shows that 3 liters of water leak out of the barrel every hour. At this rate, the barrel will be empty after 33 hours and 20 minutes. Note that after 24 hours, the line in the graph changes from solid to dashed. That is because the data only go up to 24 hours. A measurement beyond 24 hours is a *projection,* or guess.

Suppose the barrel holds 120 liters of water. How long would it take for all the water to leak from the barrel?

The barrel loses 3 liters of water every hour:

$$120 \text{ liters} \div 3 \text{ liters/hour} = 40 \text{ hours}$$

It would take 40 hours for all 120 liters to leak from the barrel.

It's Your Turn

Please read each question carefully. For each multiple-choice question, circle the letter of the correct response.

1 **Which part of this swamp ecosystem is least likely to change throughout the year?**

   A   the kinds of animals hunting for food there

   B   the colors of the leaves on the trees

   C   the types of trees growing in the swamp

   D   the temperature of the water

2 **Which of these changes could you best describe by measuring mass?**

   A   the path of a ball

   B   the growth of a caterpillar

   C   the movement of a pinwheel

   D   the loss of leaves from a tree

3 Monsoons are wind patterns in some parts of the world. In India, monsoons bring a lot of rain in summer months. They bring very little rain in winter months. Which of the following best describes the pattern in monsoons?

A They repeat every year.

B They repeat every month.

C They repeat every week.

D They repeat every day.

Base your answers to questions 4 and 5 on the table below and on your knowledge of science.

AVERAGE HIGH TEMPERATURES IN A TOWN

Year	Season	Average High Temperature
1	winter (December to February)	7°C
1	spring (March to May)	14°C
1	summer (June to August)	26°C
1	fall (September to November)	15°C
2	winter (December to February)	6°C
2	spring (March to May)	14°C
2	summer (June to August)	25°C
2	fall (September to November)	15°C

4 A student recorded the average high temperature in her town during each season for two years. The table above shows her data. What will the high temperature most likely be in the summer of year 3?

A 26°C

B 18°C

C 30°C

D 15°C

For this open-ended question, write your answers on the lines.

5 Describe the pattern in the student's data.

_____

_____

UNIT 2 Analysis, Inquiry, and Design, Part 2

Engineering and Design

Major Understandings 1T1.1a–c; 1T1.3a–c; 1T1.5c; 6KI6.1, 2

Engineers use science to solve problems. They follow a common set of steps to design or redesign objects. Cars, computers, telephones, sewers, bridges, and toys are all things that engineers design.

Identifying Problems

Whether engineers are designing roads, glue, rockets, mobile phones, or roller coasters, they are solving problems. To solve a problem, engineers might make something work better. For example, they might try to make a computer work faster. They might also solve a problem by making something new. For example, they might make a new kind of seat belt that keeps people safe in cars.

The first step to designing a better product is identifying a problem to solve. Most things you use every day have some features that make them hard to use. For example, suppose Maria takes a lunch to school every day. She carries her lunch in a metal lunch box. The lunch box is light and small, but it does not keep her food cold. She can use engineering to find a way to keep her lunch cool.

Proposing Solutions

After an engineer identifies a problem, he or she will think of different ways to solve the problem. Engineers use science ideas when thinking of solutions. They must first learn what is causing the problem. Then, they can start to think of ways to solve it.

To start solving her lunch box problem, Maria does some research. She wants to learn more about why her lunch does not stay cool.

Maria learns from her research that some materials, such as metal, let heat move through them easily. These materials are called *conductors*. Other materials do not let heat move through them easily. These materials are called *insulators*. To keep something cold, you have to keep it *insulated* so that heat from the environment does not warm it up.

> An **engineer** is someone who solves problems using science.

> When a material transfers heat, scientists say that the material *conducts* heat. Metal is a good conductor of heat. This is why it is dangerous to touch any hot metal, such as a pan on a stove.

Which of the following would most likely help keep Maria's lunch cool during the day?

A adding a heavier material to her lunch box

B adding a conducting material to her lunch box

C adding heat to her lunch box

D adding an insulating material to her lunch box

> Adding heat to the lunch box would make the box warmer, so choice C is incorrect. Adding a conducting material will let heat move into the lunch box more easily. That will make her lunch warmer, so choice B is incorrect. Adding a heavier material might keep the lunch cool. However, adding an insulating material will definitely help keep the lunch cool. Therefore, the correct answer is D.

Maria learns that metal is a conductor. Now she knows why her lunch gets warm. The heat from outside the lunch box moves through the box easily. It moves into her food and warms it up.

Maria also learns that rubber, Styrofoam, wool, and paper are insulators. She thinks of some ways to solve her problem. Here are three possible solutions she thinks of:

Solution 1: Wrap the lunch box with rubber, Styrofoam, wool, and paper.
Solution 2: Wrap each drink and food item inside the lunch box with paper.
Solution 3: Fill the lunch box with wool before putting the lunch in it.

Evaluating Solutions

Engineers cannot try every solution they think of. There are always **constraints.** Constraints are limits. Money is a very common constraint. For example, building walls from very thick pieces of wood can make the walls stronger. However, thick pieces of wood are very expensive. Engineers have to find solutions that are less expensive, but still strong enough to be safe. The table below shows some of the constraints on Maria's lunch box ideas.

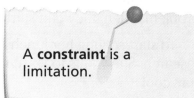

A **constraint** is a limitation.

CONSTRAINTS ON LUNCH BOX

Constraint	Description
Weight	The lunch box cannot be too heavy.
Size	The lunch box cannot be too large.
Time	The lunch box must be easy to pack.

Maria must **evaluate,** or judge, each of her solutions. She must figure out which one best fits all the constraints.

Which of Maria's three solutions will most likely fit all the constraints? Explain your answer.

If Maria wraps her lunch box in all the insulators, it will probably be very large and heavy. So, solution 1 is not the best choice. It would take a lot of time to wrap each item in the lunch box with paper. So, solution 2 is not the best choice. Filling the lunch box with wool will not take very long. The wool will not make the lunch box any bigger, and it will not weigh very much. Therefore, solution 3 is the best choice.

Testing a Solution

After engineers identify a possible solution, they test the solution to see how well it works. Before they test, they identify **criteria** for judging the solution. Criteria are specific characteristics that a product has to have. For example, Maria could use the following criteria to decide how well her lunch box solution works:

- The temperature inside the lunch box should stay below 40°F for 4 hours.
- The lunch box should have a mass of less than 0.5 kg when it is empty.

Maria tests her solution. She tapes wool socks around the inside of her lunch box. Then, she weighs the lunch box using a spring scale and records the weight. She adds her lunch and waits 4 hours. After 4 hours, she opens the lunch box slightly and measures the temperature inside with a thermometer.

Criteria are rules that you use to make a decision. A single rule is called a *criterion.*

The criteria that engineers use when solving problems can change. For example, when cars were first invented, a criterion might have been that the cars needed to go at least 30 miles per hour. Now, a criterion for a car might be that it needs to go at least 70 miles per hour.

The table below shows Maria's data.

DATA FROM TEST OF LUNCH BOX WITH WOOL LINING

Measurement	Value
Mass of lunch box and socks	0.75 kg
Temperature inside lunch box after 4 hr	38.9°F

Improving the Solution

After testing a solution, engineers study the data to see if they meet the criteria. In many cases, the first solution does not meet all of the criteria. Then, the engineers have to change the solution and test it again.

Maria's first solution did not meet all of her criteria. The inside of the lunch box stayed under 40°F. However, the empty lunch box had a mass of more than 0.5 kg. Maria decides to try out different insulators to find one that meets all of the criteria.

Maria finds rubber gloves, Styrofoam packing materials, and newspaper around her house. She decides that she will test each of these insulators. She uses the same method she used to test the wool socks. The table below shows her results.

WEIGHT AND TEMPERATURE OF LUNCH BOX WITH INSULATOR AFTER 4 HOURS

Type of Insulator	Mass of Lunch Box with Insulator	Temperature after 4 Hours
Rubber gloves	0.7 kg	43.3°F
Styrofoam	0.4 kg	39.1°F
Wool socks	0.75 kg	38.9°F
Newspaper	0.3 kg	41.7°F

Based on the table above, which insulator is the best solution?

A rubber gloves   **C** wool socks

B Styrofoam   **D** newspaper

The insulator that is the best solution is the one that meets both criteria. The rubber gloves and wool socks make the lunch box too heavy. Choices A and C are incorrect. The newspaper does not keep the food cold enough, so choice D is incorrect. The Styrofoam has a small mass and keeps the food cold, so the correct answer is B.

It's Your Turn

Please read each question carefully. For each multiple-choice question, circle the letter of the correct response.

1 **A person notices that his running shoes slip on icy sidewalks. He decides to put special covers over his shoes to make them less slippery. The shoe covers help him because they**

  A   make him less likely to fall and get hurt

  B   make it easier for him to tie his shoes

  C   help his shoes fit him better

  D   keep his feet from getting tired

2 **Which of these features would most likely make a kite difficult to fly?**

  A   very strong string

  B   very heavy fabric

  C   bright orange paint

  D   plastic supports

3 **A student's desk wobbles because one of the legs does not touch the ground. She has two pencils, two pieces of tape, and 10 sheets of paper. Which of the following actions would most likely help her fix the desk?**

  A   draw a picture of a desk with four legs that touch the floor

  B   tape the paper to the desk to push it down

  C   use the pencils to make the short leg stronger

  D   put folded-up paper under the short leg to hold it up

4 **A student wants to plant a garden. The seeds she is planting must be placed 5 cm apart. She needs to decide what shape to make her garden. Which of these garden shapes would allow her to plant the most seeds?**

  A   a rectangle 10 cm long and 2 cm wide

  B   a square with sides that are 25 cm long

  C   a rectangle 15 cm long and 5 cm wide

  D   a square with sides that are 10 cm long

Base your answers to questions 5, 6, and 7 on the table below and on your knowledge of science.

Some students want to make "egg cushions." Each cushion must have a mass of less than 0.25 kg. Each student makes a cushion. Each cushion is made of a different material. The students place an egg in each cushion. Then, they drop each cushion from a height of 5 meters. The table below shows their observations.

TESTS OF EGG CUSHIONS

Type of Material	Mass of Egg Cushion	Did the egg crack?
Cotton balls	0.21 kg	no
Bubble wrap	0.19 kg	yes
Kitchen sponge	0.29 kg	no
Tissues	0.15 kg	yes

5 **Which of the following was most likely a criterion for this experiment?**

A   The cushion must keep the egg from cracking.

B   The cushion must allow the egg to crack only a little bit.

C   The cushion must be able to fall 5 meters.

D   The cushion must allow the egg to fall out easily.

6 **The student who made the cushion from tissues wants to improve his design. The best way for him to improve his design would be to**

A   remove some tissues from the cushion

B   drop the cushion from a lower height

C   put cotton balls in the cushion

D   replace the tissues with bubble wrap

For this open-ended question, write your answers on the lines.

7 **Based on the criteria and constraints, which of the egg cushions was the best? Give two pieces of information that support your answer.**

_____

_____

_____

Hands-On Lesson: Predicting

Major Understandings 1S1.1a; 1S1.3a; 1S2.3a, b; 1S3.2a; 1S3.4a; 6KI5.1

In this activity, you will make a simple **pendulum** by tying a metal washer to a string. You will predict how changing the length of the string will affect the pendulum's swing.

> A **pendulum** is an object that swings back and forth from a fixed point.

Materials

- 3 × 5 index card
- ruler
- hole punch
- new, unsharpened pencil
- tape
- desk or table
- metal washer
- spool of string
- scissors
- stopwatch

Part I: Setting Up the Pendulum

1 Use the ruler to draw a straight line connecting one corner of the index card to the opposite corner. Draw another straight line connecting the other two corners to make an "X."

2 Punch a hole in the index card at the middle of the "X," where the two lines cross.

3 Tape one end of the pencil to the top of the desk or table. The other end of the pencil should stick out away from the table. It should be parallel to the ground.

4 Push the pencil through the hole in the index card until the index card touches the table. The "X" on the index card should face away from the table. You should be able to see the "X" when you look along the pencil from the side that is not taped to the table. Tape the index card to the table.

5 Tie one end of the string to the washer. Using the ruler, measure 30 cm of string from the washer. Cut the string to that length.

6 Tie the free end of the string to the free end of the pencil. Tie the knot on the pencil's underside. The string and washer should hang in front of the index card, as shown in figure 1 on the following page.

> When measuring the string, remember to line up the "0" mark on the ruler with the knot around the washer.

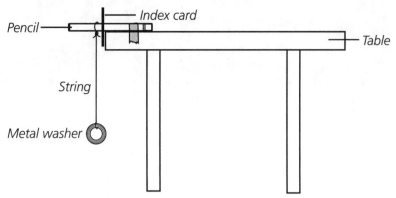

Figure 1: The string and metal washer form a simple pendulum.

Part II: Collecting Data

1 Wrap the string around the pencil four times. Use the ruler to measure the length of the string, from the bottom of the pencil to the top of the washer. Record your measurement in the first row of the table on page 77.

2 Bend or squat so you are looking along the pencil toward the "X" on the index card. Pull the washer away from the ground until the string is lined up with the bottom-left "leg" of the "X" on the index card. Use figure 2, below, as a guide. Do not pull the string toward you. Keep it parallel with the card.

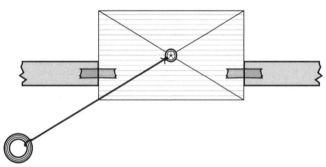

Figure 2: The string lines up with the "X" on the index card.

Why is it important to line up the string of the pendulum with the "X" on the index card?

The "X" is a guide. By lining up the string with the "X," you will release the pendulum from the same angle each time. If the angle changed from test to test, the experiment would not be controlled and your data would not reliable.

When you release the metal washer, simply let it go. Do not "push" the washer or do anything else that might affect the speed at which it falls.

3 Let go of the washer. As soon as you let go, start the stopwatch. Count the number of complete swings the pendulum makes in 10 seconds. Record your data in the first row of the table on the next page. This is test 1.

4 Repeat steps 2 and 3. This is test 2.

Number of String Wraps	Length of String (cm)	Number of Swings in 10 s (Test 1)	Number of Swings in 10 s (Test 2)
4			
8			
12			

Count one half-swing for each time the pendulum swings to the right-hand side of the index card. Count one complete swing for each time the pendulum returns to the left-hand side of the index card.

5 Wrap the string four more times around the pencil and measure the length of the string. Repeat steps 2–4. Record your data in the second row of the table.

6 Wrap the string four more times around the pencil and measure the length of the string. Repeat steps 2–4. Record your data in the third row of the table.

Question 1: How did changing the length of the string affect the number of complete swings your pendulum made?

_____

_____

_____

Question 2: Based on the data you collected, what can you conclude about the relationship between a pendulum's length and how fast it swings?

_____

_____

_____

Part III: Making and Testing Predictions

1 Predict what will happen if you continue to change the length of the pendulum.

Question 3: How many complete swings will the pendulum make if the string is not wrapped around the pencil at all?

If the string is not wrapped around the pencil, the pendulum will

make _____ complete swings.

2 Test your prediction by unwrapping the string from the pencil and repeating steps 2–4 in Part II. Measure the length of the string when it is not wrapped around the pencil. Perform two tests and record your data in the fourth row of the table on page 77.

Question 4: How many complete swings will the pendulum make if the string is wrapped 16 times around the pencil?

If the string is wrapped 16 times around the pencil, the pendulum

will make _____ complete swings.

3 Test your prediction by wrapping the string around the pencil 16 times and repeating steps 2–4 in part II. Measure the length of the string when it is wrapped 16 times around the pencil. Perform two tests and record your data in the fifth row of the table.

Question 5: Review your predictions in questions 3 and 4. Were they accurate? If not, explain how your predictions were inaccurate.

_____

_____

_____

Question 6: Review your conclusion in question 2. Is your conclusion supported by the data you collected in part III? _____

If not, **modify,** or revise, your conclusion so it agrees with all of your data.

_____

_____

_____

Part IV: Designing a New Experiment

1 Your simple pendulum has two parts: a string and a metal washer. So far, you have changed only the string. This has let you learn the relationship between a pendulum's length and how fast it swings. However, you can also change the pendulum's mass.

> When you **modify** something, you change it. New evidence can cause you to modify a previous conclusion.

Question 7: A student wants to investigate the relationship between a pendulum's mass and how fast it swings. How should the student modify this experiment?

_____

_____

_____

_____

Why is it important to keep the length of the pendulum constant, or unchanged, when investigating mass?

In a controlled experiment, only one variable changes. In this experiment, the changing variable is the mass of the pendulum. If the pendulum's length also changed, the experiment would not be controlled and the data would not be reliable.

Please read each question carefully. For each multiple-choice question, circle the letter of the correct response.

1 Which of these is the best example of a natural system?

A

C

B

D

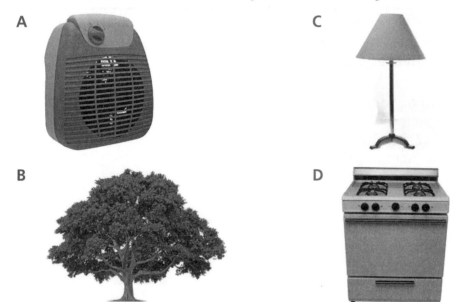

2 How is a baby doll different from a human baby?

A   The baby is alive.

B   The baby can wear clothes.

C   The doll is much bigger.

D   The doll can make sounds.

3 An engineer designs new brakes for a bicycle. The engineer most likely changed the brakes to make the bicycle

A   quieter on the road

B   faster

C   safer

D   better looking

4 A scientist is studying a snake. She sees that the snake has a pattern on its skin. The pattern looks like circles with stripes through them. Which of these is most likely the pattern on the snake's skin?

A

C

B

D

Base your answers to questions 5 and 6 on the picture below and on your knowledge of science.

The picture shows a backyard ecosystem.

5 Which of the living things in this ecosystem can grow the biggest?

  A butterfly

  B flower

  C bird

  D tree

6 Which of the following is an interaction between two living things in the ecosystem?

  A The bird eats the worm.

  B The squirrel sits on a fence post.

  C The clouds drift through the sky.

  D The tree absorbs nutrients from the soil.

7 This picture is a model of a plant.

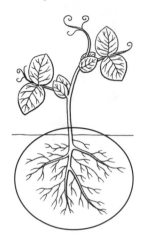

The circled part is the plant's

A roots

C leaves

B flowers

D stems

8 A student's bicycle is shown below.

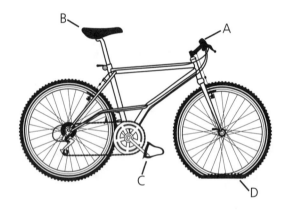

The student's bicycle is not working properly. Which part is most likely causing the bicycle not to work?

A part A

C part C

B part B

D part D

9 A student's chair makes his back hurt. He thinks of several solutions for the problem. The best solution must not cost too much money and must not disturb other students in the class. Which of the solutions below is probably best?

A get up and walk around the room every half hour

B put a small pillow on the chair to support his back

C buy a new chair

D sit on the floor instead of the chair

10 A student needs to hang a ball from the ceiling. The ball has to be at least 2.5 meters from the ceiling. She also needs the string she uses to be as <u>thin</u> as possible. Which of the following strings should she use?

A 0.5 meter of climbing rope

B 2.0 meters of fishing line

C 2.5 meters of knitting yarn

D 3.0 meters of dental floss

Base your answers to questions 11 and 12 on the graph below and on your knowledge of science.

An engineer wanted to find out how well a fan on a computer keeps the computer cool. He measured the temperature of the computer every minute. The graph shows his data.

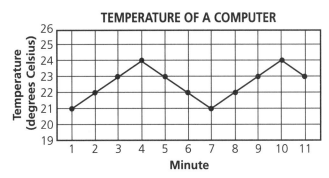

11 Based on the graph, what will the temperature most likely be in minute 12?

A 21°C

B 22°C

C 23°C

D 24°C

12 The temperature pattern repeats every

A 2 minutes

B 4 minutes

C 6 minutes

D 8 minutes

13 A farmer wants to collect data to find out which fertilizer produces the largest strawberries. When the strawberries are ripe, the farmer should

  A   measure the height of each strawberry plant with a meter stick

  B   count the number of seeds on each strawberry

  C   count the number of leaves on each strawberry plant

  D   measure the mass of each strawberry with a balance

14 A class is making a solar-powered oven. Which of the following is the best criterion for this design?

  A   The oven should be painted with five different types of paint.

  B   The oven should be big enough to roast a turkey.

  C   The oven should be able to heat to 350°F.

  D   The oven should cost at least $150 to make.

15 A student needs to carry a rock to school for a class project. The student wants to be able to use both hands while he is carrying the rock. He also wants to make sure he won't drop the rock on the ground. Which of these is the best solution for the student?

  A   carry the rock in his hand

  B   place the rock in a backpack

  C   place the rock in a plastic grocery bag

  D   hold the rock under his arm

Base your answers to questions 16 and 17 on the table below and on your knowledge of science.

A class observed the number of different birds that came to a bird feeder outside their classroom during one day. They recorded their data in this table.

TYPES OF BIRDS THAT CAME TO THE BIRD FEEDER

Type of Bird	Number at 8 A.M.	Number at 1 P.M.
Blue Jay	4	2
Dove	7	3
Cardinal	3	1
Finch	5	2

16 Based on the data in the table, which of these statements is true?

   A   More birds come to the feeder in the afternoon than in the morning.

   B   More birds come to the feeder in the morning than in the afternoon.

   C   There are more doves than finches near the school.

   D   There are more blue jays than cardinals near the school.

17 The students come up with explanations for their observations. Which explanation could be tested using a scientific investigation?

   A   Blue jays would rather eat late in the day.

   B   Doves like eating at the school more than finches do.

   C   Fewer cardinals live near the school than other birds.

   D   Most finches want to eat before blue jays eat.

18 A gardener wants to build a stand to hold a flowerpot. The diameter of the bottom of the flowerpot is 20 cm. The picture below shows the shape of the stand.

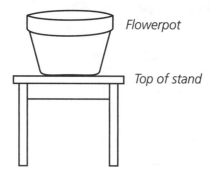

Flowerpot

Top of stand

To make the top of the stand, the gardener should use

A a square piece of wood with sides that are 30 cm long

B a rectangle of wood that is 15 cm long and 18 cm wide

C a circle of thick plastic with a diameter of 18 cm

D a triangle of thick plastic that is 15 cm long at its widest part

19 A student wanted to be able to see in the dark without having to hold a flashlight. He taped a flashlight to the side of a hat, as shown below.

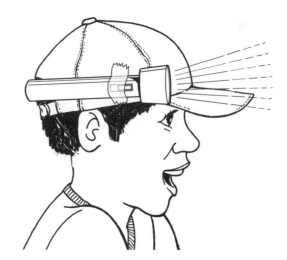

When he tested his design, he noticed that the flashlight shifted a lot when he walked. The student can most likely fix this problem by

A getting a smaller hat

B using a bigger flashlight

C using more tape to hold the flashlight to the hat

D adding a larger flashlight on the other side of the hat

Base your answers to questions 20 and 21 on the table below and on your knowledge of science.

Three students want to be able to run more quickly. In September, they timed how long it took each of them to run one mile. From September to December, each student practiced running for a different amount of time each week. In December, they timed again how long it took them to run a mile. They recorded their times in the table below.

TIME IT TOOK THREE STUDENTS TO RUN ONE MILE IN SEPTEMBER AND DECEMBER

Student	Time to Run One mile in September (min)	How Often the Student Ran Between September and December	Time to Run One Mile in December (min)
A	15	once a week	14
B	12	twice a week	10
C	13	four times a week	9

20 **Based on the table, which conclusion is most likely true?**

    A   You cannot learn how to run more quickly.

    B   You can run more quickly if you practice running more often.

    C   You can run more quickly in September than you can in December.

    D   You have to run at least four times a week to learn to run more quickly.

21 **In September, student B ran the fastest mile. She predicted that she would run the fastest mile in December. What is the most likely reason her prediction was wrong?**

    A   She practiced running more often than student A did.

    B   She took longer to run one mile in December.

    C   She ran the mile faster in December than she did in September.

    D   She did not practice running as much as student C did.

22 A student observes the number of vehicles he passes on his way to school every day for five days. On Monday, there were 5 trucks and 9 cars. Every day, the number of trucks increased by 2, and the number of cars increased by 3. Fill in the table to show the student's observations. The first column has been done for you.

NUMBER OF VEHICLES ON THE WAY TO SCHOOL

	Monday	Tuesday	Wednesday	Thursday	Friday
Trucks	5				
Cars	9				

For each open-ended question, write your answers on the lines.

23 A student is designing a bird feeder. List <u>two</u> criteria the student should use to decide if his design is good.

(1) _____

(2) _____

24 The pictures below show three different living things. Fill in the lines to describe the different sizes of the living things.

Mouse   *Elephant*   *Cat*

The _____ can never be bigger than the _____, which can

never be bigger than the _____.

25 The picture is a model of a forest ecosystem in New York State.

Based on the picture, identify <u>two</u> animals that live in this forest ecosystem.

(1) _____

(2) _____

26 Name <u>two</u> ways a maple tree can change over time. Name only natural changes.

(1) _____

(2) _____

27 A student leaves a banana in his locker on Friday afternoon. Name <u>one</u> way the banana will change over the weekend. Name <u>one</u> way the banana will stay the same.

(1) _____

(2) _____

Unit 3
The Physical Setting, Part 1

The world around us is constantly changing. Earth, the Sun, and other space objects move in patterns through the solar system. In addition, many different processes shape and change Earth's surface. In this unit, you will learn how Earth, the Sun, the Moon, and the stars move and change.

There are four lessons in this unit:

1 **Patterns of Motion in the Solar System** The Sun and many other stars are easy to see in Earth's sky. The Moon is usually easy to see, too. However, it is not easy to see how they really move. In this lesson, you will learn how the motions of Earth, the Sun, the Moon, and the stars relate to one another. You will also learn how these motions affect things that happen on Earth.

2 **The Water Cycle** Water is very important to life on Earth. Water is also important in shaping Earth's surface. In this lesson, you will learn how water moves between different water bodies, the air, and the land.

3 **Weather** The weather changes from day to day. Some days are sunny. Some days are cloudy. In this lesson, you will learn how scientists observe and describe the weather. You will also learn how scientists use tools and charts to study weather patterns.

4 **Changes on Earth's Surface** Earth's surface is constantly being worn down and built up. Most of these changes happen so slowly that you cannot see them. However, some changes happen very quickly. In this lesson, you will learn how water, wind, and natural events such as earthquakes can shape Earth's surface. You will also learn about the processes that form soil.

Patterns of Motion in the Solar System

Major Understandings 4PS1.1a–c

If you look up into the sky on a clear night, you might think that Earth is alone in the universe. In fact, Earth is closely connected to many objects in space. Earth is part of a system of planets, moons, asteroids, and dwarf planets. At the center of the system is a star, the Sun. This system, called the **solar system,** contains many objects that all move together in an orderly way.

Motions of Earth and the Moon

Every day, the Sun rises and sets. The Moon and far-off stars shine in the sky at night. It is warm in the summer, and it gets colder in the winter. These natural patterns are a part of life. The movements of Earth and the Moon around the Sun cause these patterns. Because Earth and the Moon move around the Sun, we have seasons, moon phases, and day and night.

Earth and the Moon are always moving. They both **rotate,** or spin on an axis. An **axis** is an imaginary line down the center of an object. The Moon's axis is straight up and down. Earth's axis is not straight up and down. It is tilted to the side.

Earth's axis

A **solar system** is a group of planets, moons, asteroids, and dwarf planets that move in patterns around a star.

To **rotate** is to spin on an imaginary line.

An **axis** is an imaginary line through the center of an object.

You have probably noticed that the Sun moves across the sky during the day. It looks like the Sun moves around Earth. However, the Sun does not actually move around Earth. The Sun appears to move across our sky because Earth rotates.

To understand how this works, think about sitting on a merry-go-round. As you look to the side, houses, trees, and other things seem to fly by. However, the houses and trees are not moving. Only the merry-go-round is moving. The merry-go-round is like Earth. The houses and trees are like the Sun.

UNIT 3 The Physical Setting, Part 1

© The Continental Press, Inc.   **DUPLICATING THIS MATERIAL IS ILLEGAL.**

As Earth and the Moon rotate, they also **revolve.** That means that they move in a path around other objects. These paths are called **orbits.** The Moon orbits, or revolves around, Earth. Earth orbits, or revolves around, the Sun.

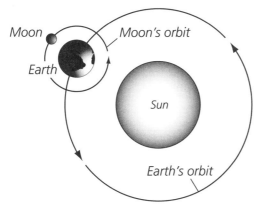

As Earth revolves around the Sun, the Moon revolves around Earth.

Which statement about the Sun and Earth is true?

  A As Earth revolves, it moves around the Sun.

  B As Earth rotates, the Sun moves around Earth.

  C As Earth revolves, the Sun moves around Earth.

  D As Earth rotates, both Earth and the Sun stay in place.

Earth's rotation makes the Sun seem to move around Earth. However, the Sun does not actually move around Earth. Therefore, choices B and C are incorrect. Earth rotates around its axis and revolves, or moves, around the Sun. Therefore, choice D is incorrect. Choice A is correct.

Days, Years, and Seasons

You have probably noticed that every year has four seasons. You have probably also noticed that the length of the day changes during a year. Earth's rotation and revolution cause both of these patterns. People use these patterns to make calendars.

As Earth spins, some areas of the planet face the Sun, and other areas face away from the Sun. It is daytime in the areas facing the Sun. It is night in the areas facing away from the Sun. One day equals the time it takes for Earth to rotate once on its axis. It takes about 24 hours for Earth to rotate once on its axis. So, one day equals about 24 hours.

The length of a year is based on Earth's revolution. It takes Earth about 365 days to make one orbit around the Sun. One orbit around the Sun equals one Earth year.

To **revolve** is to move in a path around another object.

An **orbit** is a circular path one object follows when it revolves around an object. The word *orbit* can also be used as a verb.

All the planets in the solar system revolve around the Sun, and every planet rotates on an axis. However, the planets do not all move at the same speed.

Planet	Rotation (Earth time)*
Mercury	59 days
Venus	243 days
Earth	1 day
Mars	1 day
Jupiter	10 hours
Saturn	11 hours
Uranus	17 hours
Neptune	16 hours

Planet	Revolution (Earth time)*
Mercury	3 months
Venus	7.5 months
Earth	1 year
Mars	1.9 years
Jupiter	12 years
Saturn	29.5 years
Uranus	84 years
Neptune	165 years

*These are approximations.

One year has four seasons: winter, spring, summer, and fall. We have seasons because Earth's axis is tilted. As Earth orbits the Sun, different parts of the planet face the Sun. When the top half of Earth is tilted toward the Sun, the areas on the top half have summer. This is because the top half receives more direct sunlight. Those areas heat up.

The opposite is true in winter. During winter, the top half of Earth is tilted away from the Sun. As a result, the areas on the top half receive less direct sunlight. They cool down. This is why the weather is generally warmer in summer and cooler in winter.

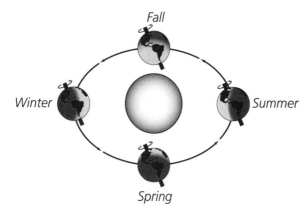

Earth's tilted axis is the reason we have seasons.

How does Earth's tilted axis affect the length of the day?

When the top half of Earth has summer, it is tilted toward the Sun. As a result, the top half faces the Sun for a greater part of Earth's rotation. This makes the day last longer. During winter, the opposite happens. The top half faces away from the Sun for a greater part of Earth's rotation. This makes the day shorter.

Moon Phases

The Moon seems to change shape from night to night. Sometimes it is a full, round ball. Other times it is just a sliver. These different shapes are called **moon phases.**

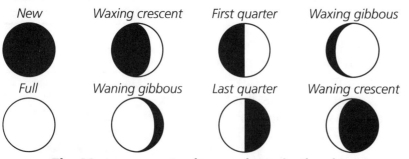

**The Moon seems to change shape in the sky.
The moon phases change during a month.**

The Moon's different shapes in the sky are called **moon phases.**

We always see the same side of the Moon from Earth. That is because the time it takes the Moon to rotate is about the same amount of time it takes the Moon to revolve.

The Moon does not actually change shape every day. The motions of Earth and the Moon around the Sun are what make the Moon seem to change shape. Unlike the Sun, the Moon does not make its own light. It reflects light from the Sun. Half of the Moon is always facing the Sun. That half of the Moon is bright. The other half is dark.

As the Moon revolves around Earth, we see different parts of the lit half of the Moon. When the Moon and the Sun are on opposite sides of Earth, we can see the entire lit half of the Moon. The Moon looks full. When the Moon is between Earth and the Sun, we can see only the dark half of the Moon. When the Moon is dark, we call it a "new" moon.

The phases of the Moon are a pattern. They repeat every 29.5 days. That is about how long a month is. In fact, the length of months is based on the moon phases. Early calendars defined months as the amount of time it took the moon to go through all of its phases. One month is about as long as it takes for the Moon to make one revolution around Earth.

Measuring Time

The movements of Earth and the Moon help people organize time into units. A year is based on Earth's revolution around the Sun. A month is about as long as the Moon's revolution around Earth. A day is equal to the time it takes for Earth to rotate once.

COMMON UNITS OF TIME

Unit	Equal to ...
Second (s)	—
Minute (min)	60 s
Hour (hr)	60 min
Day	1 rotation of Earth around its axis (about 24 hr)
Week	7 days
Month	about 1 revolution of the Moon around Earth (29.5 days)
Year	1 revolution of Earth around the Sun (about 365 days)

How many minutes are there in 1 day?

A 60

B 168

C 1,440

D 3,600

There is only one full moon in most months. When there are two full moons in one month, the second moon is called a *blue moon.* Blue moons happen very rarely. That's why the phrase "once in a blue moon" is used to refer to things that rarely happen.

People create units of time because units make it easier to talk about time. However, many units do not line up exactly with the movements of Earth and the Moon. Most months in our calendar are longer than 29.5 days. Also, Earth orbits the Sun in slightly more than 365 days. That is the reason we have leap years. Every four years, we add a day to our calendar to make up for the extra time it takes Earth to orbit the Sun.

There are 60 minutes in 1 hour, so choice A is incorrect. There are 168 hours in 1 week (24 hours/day × 7 days/week), so choice B is incorrect. There are 3,600 seconds in 1 hour (60 seconds/minute × 60 minutes/hour), so choice D is incorrect. There are 1,440 minutes in 1 day (60 minutes/hour × 24 hours/day). Choice C is correct.

We divide years, months, and days into smaller units to make it easier to keep track of time. We divide years into weeks, and we divide days into hours. For the same reason, we divide hours into minutes and seconds.

Constellations

Patterns of stars in the night sky are called **constellations.** As Earth revolves around the Sun, constellations appear in different parts of the night sky. The constellations people can see in the sky depend on where Earth is in its orbit. For example, during the winter in New York, you have to look south to see the constellation Orion. During the fall, you have to look southeast. Constellations also look different to people living in different places on Earth.

A **constellation** is a group of stars that forms a pattern.

The Greeks thought the shape of one group of stars looked like a hunter. They named the constellation "Orion," after a hunter in Greek mythology. The Lakota, a Native American tribe, saw Orion's belt as the bottom of a chief's hand.

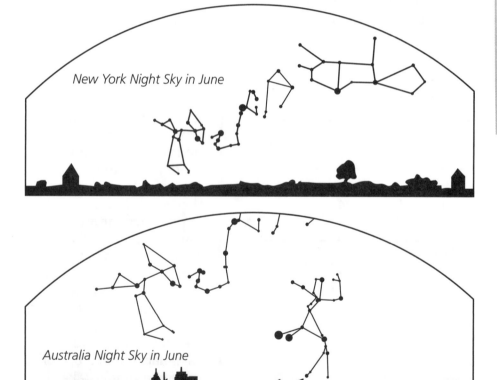

New York Night Sky in June

Australia Night Sky in June

These star maps show that constellations look different when seen from different parts of Earth at the same time of year.

Constellations also seem to move across the night sky throughout the night. Actually, the constellations themselves are not moving. They only seem to move because Earth is rotating.

96

Padma looks at the night sky just after sunset. She notices a constellation near the horizon. Later that night, the same constellation is higher in the sky. Explain why this happened.

Constellations seem to move because Earth is rotating. As Earth rotates, different constellations become visible during the night. So, Earth's rotation makes the constellations seem to move.

Please read each question carefully. For each multiple-choice question, circle the letter of the correct response.

1 **The picture shows Earth's orbit around the Sun.**

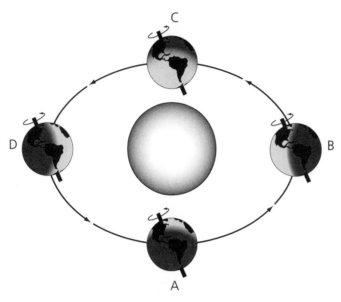

When it is winter in New York, Earth is closest to

A position A

B position B

C position C

D position D

2 **Which characteristic of a constellation changes with the seasons?**

A its apparent shape

B its location in the night sky

C the types of stars in it

D the number of stars in it

3 **A student wants to know how long it will take the flower seeds he has planted to bloom. What unit of time is best for him to use?**

A seconds

B minutes

C weeks

D years

For this open-ended question, write your answer on the line.

4 **Suppose Earth took 200 days to revolve once around the Sun. How long would a year be on Earth?**

_____ days

The Water Cycle

Major Understandings 4PS2.1c; 4LE6.2c

You can find water in many different places on Earth. Water can be in oceans, lakes, rivers, and other water bodies. It can also be in clouds, rain, snow, and ice. There is even water that you can't see in the air.

Water can be a solid, liquid, or gas. All water on Earth can change between these three states. As it changes, it moves all around the planet.

The Water Cycle

The water you see on Earth today is the same water that was on Earth millions of years ago. The water on Earth is constantly moving, from water bodies to clouds, rain, and snow. Earth's water moves in a cycle called the **water cycle.** You can find water in all steps of the cycle at any time on Earth.

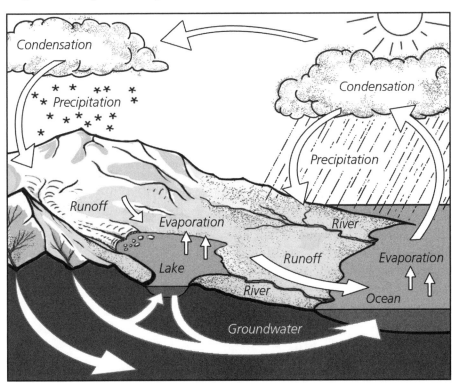

Water moves all around Earth through the water cycle.

Remember that water can be a solid, liquid, or gas. When water is a gas, it is called **water vapor.** Water vapor is in the air all around you. When water vapor cools, it changes from a gas to a liquid. This process is called **condensation.**

The **water cycle** is the path water takes as it moves between the oceans, the land, and the air. Water is constantly moving through the water cycle.

The water cycle is a system because it is made up of many parts. It is also a pattern because it repeats in a cycle.

When water is a gas, it is called **water vapor.**

During **condensation**, a gas changes into a liquid.

The glass below is filled with ice water. Explain how condensation causes water droplets to form on the outside of the glass.

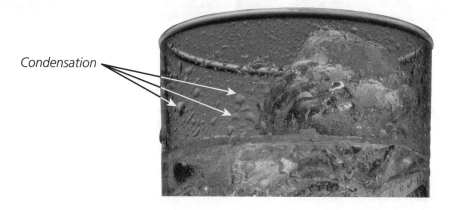

Condensation

Water vapor in the air touches the cold glass and cools. As the water vapor cools, it changes from a gas to a liquid. The liquid water collects in droplets on the outside of the glass.

When water vapor cools, it condenses into liquid droplets. If enough droplets high in the air collect in one area, they form a cloud. When a lot of water condenses into clouds, the drops become heavy. Eventually, the clouds can no longer hold the water droplets. The drops fall to Earth's surface. Water falling to Earth's surface is called **precipitation.**

Precipitation can be rain, which is liquid water. Precipitation can also be snow, sleet, or hail. These are different kinds of frozen, or solid, water.

Energy from the Sun heats bodies of water. This heat causes water to change from a liquid to a gas. This process is called **evaporation.** The water vapor rises into the air. Eventually, some of the water vapor in the air condenses and forms clouds. In this way, the water cycle repeats.

Remember that water vapor is an invisible gas. It is in the air all around us, but we cannot see it. When you see water in the air, such as steam rising from a teapot, you are seeing tiny drops of liquid water, not water vapor.

Precipitation is liquid or solid water falling to Earth's surface.

During **evaporation,** a liquid changes into a gas.

A boy sees a puddle after a rainstorm. The next day, the puddle is smaller. The water in the puddle probably

A condensed

B evaporated

C became colder

D became dirtier

Condensation happens when water turns from a gas into a liquid. The water in the puddle is already liquid, so choice A is incorrect. If the water became colder or dirtier, it would not make the puddle smaller. So, choices C and D are incorrect. Evaporation happens when a liquid turns into a gas. If some of the liquid in the puddle evaporated, the puddle would become smaller. The correct choice is B.

When water falls as precipitation, some of it sinks into the ground. **Groundwater** is water that is below the ground. Most groundwater is found in rocks and soil. Groundwater can stay underground or it can move through the ground to water bodies such as lakes and oceans. Some water that falls as precipitation flows over the land. This water is called **runoff.** Runoff flows over Earth's surface into bodies of water.

Which of the following statements is true?

A There is more water on Earth now than there was millions of years ago.

B There is less water on Earth now than there was millions of years ago.

C There is the same amount of water on Earth now as there was millions of years ago.

The water on Earth constantly moves from one place to another. In other words, it is recycled. However, the processes in the water cycle do not make or destroy water. Therefore, the total amount of water on Earth is not changing very much. The correct answer is C.

Groundwater is water within rocks and soil underground. Water in wells is also groundwater.

Runoff is water that flows over land instead of soaking into the ground.

Most questions on the New York State science test have four answer choices. However, a few questions on the test only have three answer choices, like this question has.

What Powers the Water Cycle?

The Sun is what keeps water moving through the water cycle. The Sun's energy heats bodies of water, causing water to rise into the air as water vapor. Without this water vapor, clouds would not form and there would be no precipitation. Without precipitation, runoff would not collect. So, without the Sun, the water cycle could not happen.

It's Your Turn

Please read each question carefully. For each multiple-choice question, circle the letter of the correct response.

1 Look at the picture below.

This picture shows

A runoff

B evaporation

C precipitation

D condensation

2 Which statement best describes what causes water to change from a liquid to a gas in the water cycle?

A Cold air cools water vapor in the sky.

B The Sun heats water on Earth's surface.

C Strong winds move clouds over the ocean.

D Runoff flows quickly along Earth's surface.

For this open-ended question, write your answers on the lines.

3 This diagram shows the water cycle.

Pick any <u>two</u> of the letters in the diagram. Describe what each letter represents.

(1) _____

_____

(2) _____

_____

Weather

Major Understandings 4PS2.1a, b; 4PS3.1d

The **weather** changes from day to day. Some days it is cloudy and rainy. Other days it is sunny and warm. People use tools to observe and predict weather. They can also predict weather by looking at the clouds in the sky.

Describing and Measuring Weather

People describe weather in many different ways. One of the most common ways is temperature. Sometimes people describe temperature using words such as *hot* or *cold*. People also use tools called *thermometers* to measure temperature exactly.

A weather thermometer measures the temperature of the air. When air heats the liquid inside the thermometer, the liquid expands and moves up the tube. The tube has a scale on the side to show the temperature. In the metric system, temperature is measured in degrees Celsius (°C). However, many people also measure temperature in degrees Fahrenheit (°F). The following table lists some important temperatures in the metric and nonmetric systems.

	°C	°F
Water freezes at …	0	32
The average temperature of Earth's surface is …	13.9	56.9
The average temperature of the human body is …	36.8	98.2
Water at sea level boils at …	100	212

A scientist in Buffalo measured the temperature on a snowy winter day. Which temperature did he most likely record?

A −5°C **C** 32°C

B 14°C **D** 60°C

To find the answer, look in the table above. All the answer choices are in degrees Celsius. Therefore, you should look for the answer in the column labeled "°C." On a snowy day, the temperature must be below freezing. Water freezes at 0°C. Choice A is correct.

Weather is what is happening to the outside air at a particular moment.

Many people think that a person's body is the same temperature all the time, unless the person has a fever. In fact, your body temperature changes all day. It is usually lowest in the early morning and highest in the afternoon.

Another common way to describe the weather is whether there is precipitation. Remember, *precipitation* is liquid or solid water falling to Earth's surface. Liquid precipitation is rain. Solid precipitation can be snow, sleet, or hail.

Scientists use a **rain gauge** to measure the amount of rain that has fallen. A rain gauge is a clear tube with a scale on the side. The scale helps scientists measure the amount of rain easily. The scale shows the amount of rain in millimeters or inches.

Another important part of weather is the speed and direction of the wind. Knowing the speed and direction of the wind can help a scientist predict whether a storm will come into an area. Wind speed is usually described in kilometers per hour (kph), meters per second (mps), or miles per hour (mph).

Scientists look at a **weather vane** to see which direction the wind is blowing from. Weather vanes have north, south, east, and west arms. As the wind blows, an arrow above the arms points in the direction the wind is blowing from.

Clouds and Weather

One way that people can observe and predict weather is by looking at the clouds. Remember that clouds form when water vapor in the air forms tiny droplets of water. Clouds come in many different shapes. When you know what weather different clouds bring, you can predict the weather, too.

Stratus clouds are thick, flat clouds. They form low in the sky and block out the Sun. Stratus clouds bring cooler, overcast days. **Cirrus clouds** form high in the sky. They are wispy and look like feathers. Sunlight can pass through them. You may see cirrus clouds on sunny days. **Cumulus clouds** look like puffy cotton balls. They float low in the sky on warm, sunny days.

If it is a windy and damp day, a cumulus cloud can turn into a **cumulonimbus cloud.** Cumulonimbus clouds bring thunder and rain. They can also cause hailstorms and tornadoes.

A **rain gauge** measures the amount of rain that falls.

A **weather vane** shows the direction that the wind is coming from.

Stratus clouds are thick, flat clouds that form low in the sky.

Cirrus clouds are thin, wispy clouds that form high in the sky.

Cumulus clouds are low, puffy clouds that form on sunny days.

Cumulonimbus clouds are cumulus clouds that bring thunderstorms and rain.

Stratus clouds

Cirrus clouds

Cumulus clouds

Cumulonimbus clouds

Recording and Predicting Weather

Graphs and charts help scientists study how weather changes over time. They also help scientists predict weather. Most of the time, weather happens in patterns. A **weather pattern** is weather that repeats in a predictable way.

Scientists use tools to gather weather data. Once they gather the data, they record those data. It can be hard to see patterns by just looking at numbers on a page. Scientists use weather data to make graphs and charts. Graphs and charts help scientists find patterns they might not see just by looking at data.

Scientists look for changes in temperature, wind direction, and precipitation that happen the same way over time. For example, more rain may fall in October than in any other month four years in a row. Using those data, scientists can predict that October will be the rainiest month of the next year. Graphs and charts can show how weather changes over time.

> When weather repeats in a predictable way, it is a **weather pattern.**

The graph below shows how temperatures in New York City changed over two years.

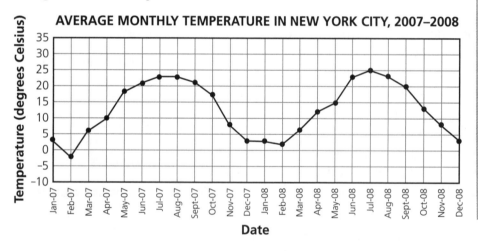

AVERAGE MONTHLY TEMPERATURE IN NEW YORK CITY, 2007–2008

> Australia has a very different weather pattern than the United States. Australia experiences its hottest days during December and its coldest days during June and July.

Based on the pattern shown in the graph, describe how the temperature in New York City likely changed during 2009.

If 2009 was similar to the other two years, the average monthly temperature continued to fall through January or February. It then probably began to rise until July. At that point, it began to fall once more. Average temperatures throughout the year were probably between -5°C and 25°C.

It's Your Turn

Please read each question carefully. For each multiple-choice question, circle the letter of the correct response.

1 A student wants to describe the weather outside her school on a certain day at lunchtime. One thing she should do is

A measure the temperature of the outside air

B find out the average amount of rain the school gets in a year

C count the number of sunny days in the last week

D predict the type of clouds that will be in the sky next week

2 A scientist describes how much rain an area gets. Which of these units does the scientist least likely use?

A millimeters

C yards

B inches

D centimeters

For this open-ended question, write your answers on the lines.

3 The picture below shows the weather in an area.

Write <u>two</u> words that a scientist would probably use to describe the weather shown in the picture. Then, identify the tool the scientist would use to measure the temperature of the air.

(1) The weather is _____ and _____.

(2) The scientist would use _____.

Changes on Earth's Surface

Major Understandings 4PS2.1d, e

Many things can change Earth's surface. Some of these changes happen slowly. For example, water and wind can take millions of years to carve a canyon through rock. Other changes can happen quickly. For example, tornadoes can knock down trees and houses in just a few seconds.

Weathering and Erosion

Water and wind are important forces in changing Earth's surface. Flowing water can break off pieces of rock. Ice that forms in rock cracks can also break rock apart as the ice expands. Wind blowing can slowly wear away at a cliff. These are examples of **weathering.** Weathering causes rocks to break into smaller pieces called **sediment.** Sand, clay, and gravel are examples of sediment.

When a rock breaks down into sediment, the sediment does not usually stay in the same place. Instead, water, wind, and gravity may move it. For example, ocean waves can pick up sand and carry it out to sea. This is an example of **erosion.** Erosion is the movement of sediment.

Weathering is a process that breaks down rock into smaller pieces.

Pieces of rock and soil are known as **sediment.** Sediment can include pieces of many different sizes, from tiny clay bits to huge boulders.

Erosion is the process of moving sediment over Earth's surface.

Weathering and erosion will most likely make these mountains

A taller

B shorter

C stronger

D harder

Weathering and erosion break down rock and carry it away. If the rock on the mountains breaks down, the mountains will become shorter. The correct answer is B.

In most places on Earth, water causes the most erosion. Fast-moving water can carry sediment for very long distances. Even slow-moving water can carry tiny sediments, such as clay.

Wind can also cause erosion. Wind can carry tiny sediments through the air. Wind erosion is usually important only in deserts and other very dry places.

Gravity can also cause erosion. Gravity is a force that pulls objects toward Earth's surface. Gravity pulls rock at the top of a hill toward the bottom of the hill. That pull can cause the rock to slide down the hill.

> Gravity helps cause most kinds of erosion. Gravity causes rivers to flow downhill. Gravity also causes rock falls and landslides that erode mountainsides quickly.

Deposition

Rivers carry sediment over Earth's surface, so they cause erosion. When a river reaches the ocean, it slows down. As the river slows, the sediment it is carrying sinks. The sediment builds up and forms a *delta*. A river forming a delta is an example of **deposition.** Deposition is the process in which sediment is laid down onto Earth's surface.

> **Deposition** is the process of dropping sediment that has been carried from another place.

Erosion and deposition may happen in the same place. For example, many rivers have curves in them. On the inside of a curve in a river, deposition happens. On the outside of the curve, erosion happens. Over time, the combined erosion and deposition can make the river curvier and longer.

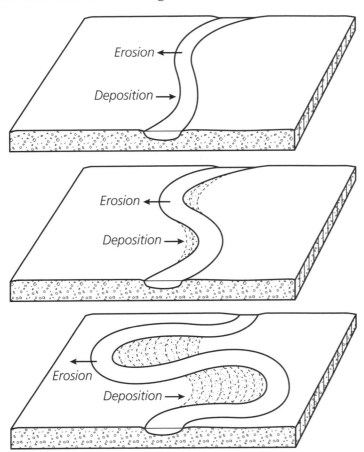

Soil

Weathering breaks rock down into smaller pieces. Many of these rock pieces become part of soil. **Soil** is the loose material that covers the ground in many places. Below the soil is solid rock called *bedrock*.

Soil is made of sediment and the remains of dead plants and animals. These remains look black and spongy. Most soil also contains water, air, and many living things. If you use a hand lens to look closely at a sample, you can see the different parts that make up soil.

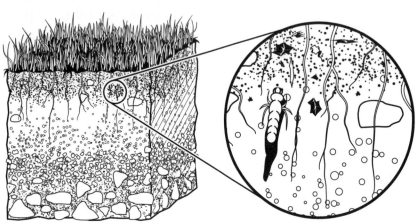

Soil contains pieces of rocks and minerals, water, air, and pieces of dead plants and animals.

Natural Events

Natural events can also change Earth's surface. These natural events can help or harm living things. Floods, hurricanes, fires, earthquakes, and volcanoes are examples of natural events that can change Earth's surface.

For example, you learned that rivers carry sediment downstream to the ocean. When an area receives a large amount of rain, the river may flood. During a flood, the waters of a river spill over the banks. When this happens, sediment sinks out of the water onto the land near the river. Floods can deposit important nutrients on the soil near a river. This process happens over a few days.

Flooding can help build up land quickly, but it can also destroy it. The rushing water of a flood can weather and erode chunks of land as well as uproot trees. Floods can quickly change a landscape and kill many organisms in the flooded area.

When the weather is calm, ocean waves and currents erode the shore slowly. During a strong storm such as a hurricane, winds whip up ocean waves. The winds make the waves much larger and more powerful. These powerful waves quickly erode the shore at one place and deposit sediment in another place.

Strong storms that happen over land can also change Earth's surface. Lightning from thunderstorms can start fires in forests and grasslands. These fires can clear away dead trees. The remains of dead plants can add nutrients to the soil. However, fires also can kill living things and destroy their habitats.

Events that happen below the ground can also quickly change Earth's surface. An **earthquake** happens when rock on or below Earth's crust breaks. Rocks on either side of the break, or *fault*, move. This movement makes the surface of Earth shake. This shaking is called an earthquake. The shaking can cause damage to Earth's surface.

In most earthquakes, the rock on either side of the break doesn't move very far. However, the movement can affect areas far away. This is because the energy of an earthquake can travel thousands of kilometers. This energy can cause landslides and rock falls.

Volcanoes are openings on the surface where molten rock, called *lava*, comes out of Earth's interior. Some volcanoes are calm and erupt slowly for many years. Other volcanoes erupt suddenly and violently. They can blast rock, gases, ash, and lava quickly out over the landscape.

Volcanic eruptions can change Earth's surface over days, months, or a few years. A few years may seem like a long time, but it is a very short time compared to the millions of years it takes mountains to form.

A volcanic eruption happens near a forest. Describe <u>one</u> negative effect the eruption could have on the living things in the forest. Describe <u>one</u> positive effect the eruption could have. Be specific.

Volcanic eruptions can give off melted rock, ash, and dust. The melted rock, or lava, is very hot. If it flows into the forest, it could burn trees and other living things in the forest. The ash the volcano gives off will fall to the ground over time. The ash contains many nutrients. When it mixes with the soil, it can add nutrients to the soil. The nutrients can help plants grow better.

When rock on or below Earth's crust breaks and moves, Earth's surface shakes. This process is called an **earthquake.**

A **volcano** is an opening on Earth's surface through which ash, dust, gas, and melted rock escape.

Just how fast is fast? Think about the time spans in the chart below. Which changes on Earth's surface are rapid and which changes are slow?

CHANGES ON EARTH'S SURFACE

Event	How long does it take?
Mountain formation	Millions of years
Volcano erupting	Days to years
Flooding	Days to weeks
Hurricane	Hours
Earthquake	Seconds to minutes

It's Your Turn

Please read each question carefully. For each multiple-choice question, circle the letter of the correct response.

1 Erosion happens in a stream when water

    A soaks into the sediment in the bank

    B washes dead leaves up onto the bank

    C carries sediment away from the bank

    D lays new sediment on top of the bank

2 Hurricanes can negatively affect people because they can

    A cause houses to flood   **C** make volcanoes erupt

    B move quickly across the ocean   **D** occur in the summer

3 The picture below shows a river.

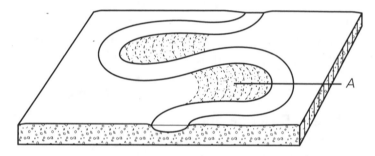

What is happening at point *A*?

    A The river is breaking down the bank.   **C** Sediment is being carried away.

    B The river is moving very quickly.   **D** Sediment is being laid down.

For this open-ended question, write your answers on the lines.

4 A student is studying the soil near his school. He studies a sample of soil with a hand lens. Name <u>three</u> things he is likely to see in the soil.

    (1) _____

    (2) _____

    (3) _____

UNIT 3 The Physical Setting, Part 1

Please read each question carefully. For each multiple-choice question, circle the letter of the correct response.

1 Scientists think that Earth's rotation is becoming slower with time. In hundreds of millions of years, Earth will take longer to rotate than it does today. When this happens,

A   Earth's day will be less than 24 hours long

B   Earth's day will be more than 24 hours long

C   Earth's year will be less than 365 days long

D   Earth's year will be more than 365 days long

2 Suppose Earth's axis were tilted more than it is. What would be the most likely result?

A   The days would be shorter.

B   The months would be longer.

C   The seasons would be more different.

D   The moon phases would be more similar.

3 When water condenses, it changes from

A   a gas to a solid

B   a liquid to a gas

C   a gas to a liquid

D   a liquid to a solid

4 A scientist recorded the wind speed near his home. Which units would he least likely use?

A   miles per hour

B   inches per second

C   meters per second

D   kilometers per hour

5 A scientist notices that the rocks along a shoreline are much smoother than they appear in pictures taken 100 years ago. Which of the following best explains this observation?

    A   water fell from clouds

    B   water picked up sediment

    C   water broke off pieces of rock

    D   water dropped sediment in a new place

Base your answers to questions 6 and 7 on the table below and on your knowledge of science.

A student records the weather in Cortland every two hours for several days. He notices a pattern in the weather. The table shows his observations.

WEATHER IN CORTLAND, NY

Time	Weather
8:00 A.M.	cool; no clouds; moist air
10:00 A.M.	warm; a little cloudy; moist air
12:00 noon	hot; very cloudy; very moist air
2:00 P.M.	very warm; raining; thunder and lightning; dark clouds
4:00 P.M.	warm; no clouds; dry air

6 What can the student conclude about the weather in the place where he made his observations?

    A   It is warmer in the mornings than it is in the afternoons.

    B   The air is drier in the mornings than in the afternoons.

    C   Thunderstorms happen when the weather is very cool and dry.

    D   It is cooler and drier after a thunderstorm than before a thunderstorm.

7 What could the student do to describe the weather more accurately?

    A   describe what Cortland looks like

    B   state what moon phase is showing at night

    C   measure the temperature of the air at different times

    D   compare the weather in Cortland to the weather somewhere else

8 A student drew a picture showing what a constellation looked like at 9:00 P.M. in March. Then, she drew a second picture with her prediction of what the constellation would look like at 9:00 P.M. in November.

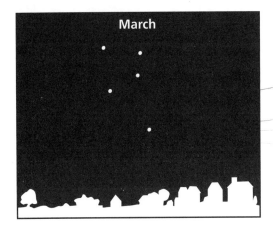
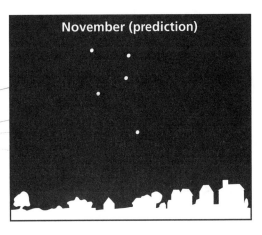

March

November (prediction)

Which of these best describes the error the student made?

A   The stars would probably be brighter in November.

B   The stars would probably be closer together in November.

C   The constellation would probably have a different number of stars in November.

D   The constellation would probably be in a different position in the sky in November.

For each open-ended question, write your answers on the lines.

9 The diagram shows the water cycle.

What is the main source of energy for the water cycle?

_____Sun_____ is the main source of energy for the water cycle.

10 The picture shows a flood.

**Describe <u>one</u> positive effect and <u>one</u> negative effect the flood
will probably have on living things in the area.**

One positive effect the flood will probably have is _the plants get
water._

One negative effect the flood will probably have is _the animals home._

Unit 4
The Physical Setting, Part 2

Physical sciences have to do with what things are made of and how things move. Physical scientists also study how energy affects things. In this unit, you will learn about matter and energy. You will also learn about different forces, such as magnetism.

There are six lessons in this unit:

1 **Matter and Its Properties**   Almost everything on Earth is made of matter. In this lesson, you will learn what matter is and how it can change. You will also learn some of the properties of matter, such as mass and volume.

2 **States of Matter**   Matter exists in three main states: solid, liquid, and gas. In this lesson, you will learn about the properties of these states of matter. You will also learn what can cause matter to change state.

3 **Energy**   There are many different kinds of energy. In this lesson, you will learn about different kinds of energy. You will also learn how energy changes from one form to another. Finally, you will learn how humans use these changes to help them do different things.

4 **Interactions of Energy and Matter**   Energy can change from one form to another. Energy can also cause changes in matter. In this lesson, you will learn how energy affects matter in ways that both help and harm people.

5 **Forces and Motion**   Objects can move in different ways. Forces cause objects to speed up and slow down. Forces also cause objects to change direction. In this lesson, you will learn how scientists describe the motions of objects. You will also learn how forces can change motion.

6 **Hands-On Lesson: Electricity and Magnetism**   Electricity and magnetism affect objects in important ways. In this hands-on lesson, you will study how electricity and magnetism affect different materials. You will also study how distance can change a magnet's effect.

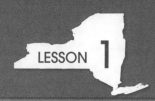

Matter and Its Properties

Major Understandings 4PS3.1a–c; 4PS3.1e–g; 4PS4.1c

Almost everything in the world around you is made of matter. Matter is "stuff." What is matter? How do you tell one substance from another?

Matter

Anything that has mass and takes up space is made of **matter.** The mass of something tells you how much matter it is made of. Almost everything you can see and feel is made of matter. Because matter takes up space, two pieces of matter cannot be in the same place at the same time. If your friend is sitting in a seat, you cannot also sit there because your friend takes up all the space on the seat.

Everything in this picture is made of matter.

Some things you cannot see are also made of matter. You cannot see air, and you usually cannot feel it, but air is made of matter. When you feel the wind, you are feeling the matter that makes up air. Some things you know about are not matter. Light and other forms of energy are not matter. They do not have mass or take up space.

Observing Properties of Matter

Each substance has its own **properties.** Some properties can be observed with your senses. Such properties are color, hardness, odor, sound, and taste. These properties can help you identify an object. They can also help you to group objects that are similar.

Matter is anything that has mass and takes up space.

Scientists call different types of matter *substances.* A solid piece of matter is called an *object.*

Properties are things you can measure or describe.

The colors of some substances or objects can help you identify them. You can generally tell copper from gold because copper is a deeper orange color. Lemons and limes have similar shapes. However, a ripe lemon is yellow, and a ripe lime is green. You can tell grape juice from milk because grape juice is purple.

Similarly, the hardness of some materials can help you tell them apart. The hardness of a solid describes how easy it is to scratch. Hard substances, such as glass and diamond, are difficult to scratch. Softer substances, such as wood, are easier to scratch.

You can observe the odor of a substance when you smell it. This can help you tell the difference between substances that may look the same. For example, water and ammonia are both clear fluids. However, water does not have an odor. Ammonia has a strong odor.

Some substances have a very particular taste. The taste of a substance can help you identify it. It can also help you learn something about what the substance is made of. If a cake tastes very sweet, you might guess that it has a lot of sugar in it.

The sound something makes is also a property you can observe. Musical instruments make certain sounds when a person plays them. You can hear that a guitar sounds different from a piano, a trumpet, or a drum.

A student is studying an apple, a strawberry, a lemon, a pretzel, a potato chip, a red chili pepper, and a green jalapeño pepper. She wants to sort them according to their properties. List <u>two</u> ways that she could sort the foods.

Think about the different properties of each food. Each food has a certain color. Therefore, the student could sort the foods by color:

    red: apple, strawberry, red chili pepper
    yellow: lemon, potato chip
    green: green jalapeño pepper
    brown: pretzel

The foods also have different tastes. They are sweet, sour, spicy, or salty. Therefore, the student could sort the foods by taste:

    sweet: apple, strawberry
    sour: lemon
    spicy: red chili pepper, green jalapeño pepper
    salty: pretzel, potato chip

Using Tools to Study Properties

You can use tools to measure some properties of matter. For example, you can use a ruler to measure the length of an object. The table below describes some tools you can use to measure certain properties of matter.

Property of Matter	Measurement Tool
length, width, and height	ruler
volume	graduated cylinder
mass	balance
weight	spring scale
temperature	thermometer

You can also use tools to study properties more closely. For example, you can feel the **texture** of an object using your hands. You can also study texture more closely using a hand lens, or magnifying glass.

There are some properties you cannot study without tools. For example, you must use a tool to find out if a substance is a conductor. **Conductors** are objects that heat and electricity move through easily. You cannot tell if something conducts electricity just by using your senses. You must use a tool called a *circuit tester* to find out if a substance conducts electricity.

Texture is the way an object feels. For example, a brick feels rough and bumpy. A block of ice feels smooth. The fur of a rabbit feels soft and silky. Tree sap feels sticky.

A **conductor** is a substance that carries electricity or heat.

An object or substance that is a poor conductor is called an *insulator*.

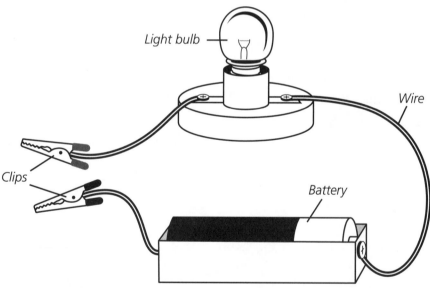

To use a circuit tester, attach both clips to the object you are testing. If the bulb lights up, the object is a conductor.

Another property you can study using tools is magnetism. If a substance sticks to a magnet, it is said to be *magnetic*. For example, iron and steel stick to magnets. In contrast, wood, plastic, and glass do not stick to magnets.

Using Properties to Identify Substances

You can use the properties of an object to help you figure out what the object is made of. For example, suppose you have a sample of a substance. You observe that it is heavy, it conducts heat, and it sticks to a magnet. Iron and steel have these properties, so you can guess that the substance is iron or steel.

The table below shows some properties of four substances.

PROPERTIES OF FOUR SUBSTANCES

Substance	Hardness	Heat Conductivity	Magnetic Attraction
Iron	hard	good	strong
Dry wood	medium	poor	none
Glass	hard	poor	none
Rubber	soft	poor	none

A student has a sample of a substance that is soft and flexible. It does not conduct heat. Based on the information in the table, the substance is most likely

A dry wood

B glass

C iron

D rubber

Dry wood and glass do not conduct heat, but they are hard. Choices A and B are incorrect. Iron is hard and conducts heat, so choice C is incorrect. Rubber is soft and flexible and does not conduct heat, so choice D is the correct answer.

Factors that Affect Properties

The properties of an object can depend on different things. Some properties, such as temperature and moisture, can depend on the environment. For example, suppose you place a penny outside on a hot, sunny day. It will become warm, and it will be dry when you touch it. But these properties will change if you place the coin outside on a cold, rainy night. It will become cold and wet.

Some properties of the penny will not change in different environments. The penny will always be made of metal. It will always be about the same shape and size.

Some of the properties of an object depend on the substances in the object. For example, most metals conduct heat and electricity well. Therefore, most objects that are made of metal conduct heat and electricity. Most kinds of wood float in water. Most objects that are made of wood also float in water.

It's Your Turn

Please read each question carefully. For each multiple-choice question, circle the letter of the correct response.

1 A student's desk is full of books.

The student wants to place a notebook inside his desk. What must he do first?

A write in the notebook

B make the notebook flatter

C make his desk smaller

D remove a book from his desk

2 A student notices that a bar magnet sticks to the refrigerator. What can she conclude about the refrigerator?

A It is cold on the inside.

B It is made of magnetic material.

C It is a conductor.

D It is heavy.

3 A student wants to study a basketball. Which of the following properties could the student observe using his hands?

A what the basketball is made of

B the color of the basketball

C the texture of the basketball

D what the basketball sounds like

4 A scientist uses a balance to measure a property of an egg. The scientist most likely measured the egg's

A mass

B width

C temperature

D color

5 This picture shows two spoons.

Metal spoon   *Wooden spoon*

Which statement about these spoons is most likely true?

A   Both spoons conduct electricity well.

B   Neither of the spoons has mass.

C   The wooden spoon is hard and the metal spoon is soft.

D   The metal spoon can conduct heat better than the wooden spoon.

For this open-ended question, write your answers in the table.

6 A student is studying the six objects shown below.

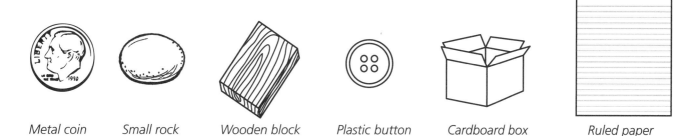

Metal coin   *Small rock*   *Wooden block*   *Plastic button*   *Cardboard box*   *Ruled paper*

The student places the objects into two groups based on their properties. Complete the table below to show how the student probably finished sorting the objects. Make sure to name the property the student used to sort the objects.

Group 1	Group 2
Property:	Property:
metal coin	wooden block
small rock	cardboard box

For this open-ended question, write your answers on the lines.

7 A student takes a sweater out of the washing machine and hangs it out in the sunshine on a hot day. List two properties of the sweater that will probably change as it hangs in the sunshine.

(1) _____   (2) _____

States of Matter

Major Understandings 4PS3.2a–c

Remember that matter is anything that has mass and volume. Most matter exists in one of three **states of matter: solid, liquid,** or **gas.**

Three States of Matter

Matter in its solid state has a *fixed,* or unchanging, volume and shape. For example, a frozen ice cube's volume and shape do not change when you take it out of the ice tray.

Matter in the liquid state has a fixed volume but not a fixed shape. For example, liquid water in a measuring cup takes the shape of the cup. When you pour the water into a mixing bowl, the water takes the shape of the bowl. However, the volume of the water does not change.

One cup of liquid

A liquid's shape can change, but its volume does not.

Matter in the gas state does not have a fixed volume or a fixed shape. When you fill balloons from a helium tank, the gas from the tank expands. The gas from a small tank can fill balloons with a larger volume than the tank. When you squeeze one of the balloons, the gas inside takes whatever shape the balloon does. **Water vapor** and other gases also expand to take the shapes of their containers.

A gas takes the shape and volume of its container.

> The **states of matter** are the physical forms that matter can take. The three most common states of matter are solid, liquid, and gas.
>
> Matter is **solid** if it has a fixed volume and shape.
>
> Matter is **liquid** if it has a fixed volume but no fixed shape.
>
> Matter is **gas** if it has no fixed volume or shape.
>
> **Water vapor** is water in the gas state.

Look at the picture of ice floating in water. Identify two states of water in the picture. Tell where each state is.

All three states of water (liquid, solid, and gas) are present in the picture. The ice is water in the solid state. The ocean water is in the liquid state. The air contains water in the gas state.

Changes of State

Matter can change from one state to another. Ice can become liquid water. Liquid water can become water vapor. Water vapor can become liquid water. Liquid water can become ice. When a substance changes from one state to another, it is called a **change of state.** Matter can change state when heat is added to it or taken away from it.

If you add enough heat to ice, it will melt into liquid water. If you add more heat to the liquid water, it will boil. During boiling, the liquid water turns into water vapor. Liquid water can also become water vapor without boiling. This process is called **evaporation.**

If you remove heat from water vapor, the vapor turns into liquid water. This is called **condensation.** You have probably seen condensation on the outside of a cold glass. When enough heat is taken away from a liquid, the liquid forms a solid. This is what happens when liquid water freezes.

A **change of state** happens when matter goes from one state to another.

Liquid water freezes when the temperature is 0°C or lower. Liquid water boils when the temperature is 100°C or higher.

Evaporation is a change from a liquid to a gas. Evaporation generally happens when heat is added to a liquid.

Condensation is the change from a gas to a liquid. Condensation generally happens when heat is removed.

When heat is added to a solid, the solid melts into a liquid. When heat is added to a liquid, the liquid evaporates into a gas.

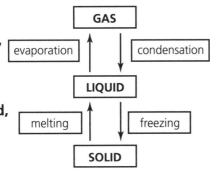

When heat is taken away from a gas, the gas condenses into a liquid. When heat is taken away from a liquid, the liquid freezes into a solid.

Which of these situations will most likely cause a change of state?

    A Ice is warmed to -1°C.

    B Water is cooled to 10°C.

    C Water is warmed to 100°C.

    D Water vapor is cooled to 101°C.

Remember, liquid water freezes at 0°C and boils at 100°C. Therefore, ice will not melt if the temperature is below 0°C. Choice A is incorrect. Water will not freeze if the temperature is above 0°C, so choice B is incorrect. Water vapor will not condense if the temperature is above 100°C, so choice D is incorrect. Choice C is the correct answer.

Changing Properties

Some properties of a substance can change. For example, a gas can be squeezed into a small container, or it can expand to fill a large one. In both cases, the volume of the gas changes. However, its mass does not change.

A student set a tray of ice cubes on a table. An hour later, the ice cubes were melted. Which property of the ice changed?

    A magnetism

    B mass

    C shape

    D state

If you place water or ice cubes near a magnet, they will not be drawn toward it. So, choice A is incorrect. A liquid can change shape if you put it in a different container. However, the melted ice stayed in the tray, and its shape did not change. So choice C is incorrect. No matter disappeared, so mass did not change. Choice B is incorrect. The ice changed state from a solid to a liquid. The correct choice is D.

It's Your Turn

Please read each question carefully. For each multiple-choice question, circle the letter of the correct response.

Note that question 1 has only three answer choices.

1 **A scientist is studying a sample of matter. The sample has a fixed volume, but it can change shape. The sample is most likely a**

A solid

B liquid

C gas

2 **A person pours melted gold into a container. The gold cools until it becomes solid. What will most likely happen when the person takes the solid gold out of the container?**

A Its volume and shape will change.

B Its shape and volume will stay the same.

C Its shape will change, but its volume will stay the same.

D Its volume will change, but its shape will stay the same.

3 **Which of the following best explains how a freezer causes water to change into ice?**

A The freezer absorbs heat from the liquid water.

B The liquid water absorbs heat from the freezer.

C The freezer causes the temperature of the water to increase.

D The water causes the temperature of the freezer to decrease.

For this open-ended question, write your answers on the lines.

4 **A scientist heats a piece of solid iron metal until it melts. Describe two ways the properties of the iron will change as it melts.**

(1) _____

(2) _____

Energy

Major Understandings 4PS4.1a, b, e, f; 4PS4.2a, b

Energy is all around you. **Energy** is the ability to do work. Without energy, nothing would move. There would be no light, sound, or heat. We would not even have any food to eat.

There are many different kinds of energy. Light, heat, electricity, sound, food, and fuel are all forms of energy. Matter can store some kinds of energy. Other kinds of energy move from place to place. In many cases, things happen when one object passes energy to another object.

Chemical Energy and Electricity

You may have heard people say that food gives you the energy you need to do things. Food contains a kind of stored energy called **chemical energy.** The nutrients that make up the food store the chemical energy. When you eat food, your body breaks down the nutrients and releases the energy. You use the energy to breathe, run, think, and even sleep.

Food is not the only material that contains chemical energy. **Fossil fuels,** such as coal and gasoline, also contain chemical energy. Fossil fuels form when dead plants and animals are buried. Over millions of years, heat and pressure change the chemicals in their bodies into fossil fuels. We burn these fuels to release the chemical energy in them. We use the energy to move our cars, heat our homes, and make electricity.

Electricity is another form of energy. We use electricity to power many of the things we use every day. We get most of our electricity by burning fossil fuels. We also get electricity from batteries. Batteries store chemical energy. They change the chemical energy to electricity.

Electricity moves through special paths called **circuits.** Circuits can have many parts. However, most circuits contain three main parts:

- a source of electricity, such as a battery
- metal wire
- a device, such as a light bulb, that does something when electricity flows through it

Energy is what makes things happen.

Chemical energy is energy that is stored in the chemicals in matter.

Fossil fuels include coal, oil, and natural gas. They formed from the remains of dead plants and animals.

A **circuit** is a path that electricity can flow through.

UNIT 4 The Physical Setting, Part 2

The picture below shows how you could connect a battery, some wire, and a light bulb to form a circuit.

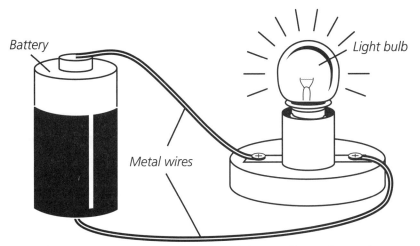

Battery

Light bulb

Metal wires

The wires are a path for electricity to flow through.

Electricity can flow only through a **closed circuit.** A closed circuit is a complete path through which electricity can flow. The circuit shown in the picture above is a closed circuit because it contains a complete loop that electricity can flow through. When electricity flows through this circuit, the light bulb will glow.

If the wire was disconnected or cut, the circuit would become an **open circuit.** An open circuit is a path that is incomplete or that has one or more gaps in it. Electricity cannot flow through an open circuit.

A **closed circuit** is a kind of circuit that contains a complete path for electricity to flow through. Electricity can flow through only closed circuits.

An **open circuit** is a kind of circuit that does not contain a complete path for electricity to flow through. Electricity cannot flow through an open circuit.

There is a small wire, called a *filament,* in the light bulb. When electricity flows through the filament, it heats up and begins to glow. That's why a light bulb lights up.

What would most likely happen if one of the wires in the circuit on this page was cut?

    A The wires would heat up.

    B The light bulb would go out.

    C The battery would lose electricity.

    D The light bulb would glow more brightly.

If one of the wires was cut, the circuit would be open. Electricity cannot flow through an open circuit. An open circuit would not cause the wires to heat up, so choice A is incorrect. Electricity can flow out of the battery only when the circuit is closed, so choice C is incorrect. The light bulb glows only when electricity moves through the circuit, so choice D is incorrect. Choice B is the correct answer.

Light and Heat

Most of the energy on Earth comes from sunlight. Light is a form of energy. Plants use light energy to make food. We can use special tools, such as solar panels, to change sunlight into electricity. Light can also make objects warmer. The air is generally warmer on a sunny day than on a cloudy day. The water in a lake or in the ocean is warmer in the summer than in the winter.

Heat is another important kind of energy. It is energy that moves from a warmer object to a cooler object. For example, if you hold an ice cube in your hand, heat will move from your hand into the ice cube.

The picture shows a fire in a fireplace.

Describe <u>two</u> ways that heat moves from one object to another in the fireplace.

> As the logs burn, heat moves from the fire to the logs. Heat also moves from the burning logs to the air in the fireplace. Both the logs and the air become warmer as heat moves into them.

There are many different ways to make heat. One way is to rub objects together. If you rub your hands together, they become warm. Systems often lose energy when their parts rub against each other and create heat. Scientists call this rubbing *friction*.

Another way to make heat is to burn things. The burning wood in the picture above produces heat. In some cases, mixing two substances together makes heat. For example, if you mix magnesium metal with an acid, the mixture becomes warm.

Kinetic Energy, Potential Energy, and Sound

Imagine putting a glass vase on a high shelf. You have to use energy to lift the vase and put it on the shelf. The vase still has that energy when it is on top of the shelf. It has potential energy. **Potential energy** is energy that objects have because of where they are located. Objects that are farther from the ground have more potential energy than objects that are nearer to the ground.

Heat is energy that moves from hot objects to cooler objects.

Sometimes friction is useful. Brakes rely on friction to slow down a moving vehicle. Other times, however, friction takes energy that the system needs to perform work.

Potential energy is the energy something has because of where it is located.

If the vase falls off the shelf, it loses potential energy. As the vase falls, its potential energy changes into **kinetic energy,** or energy of motion. Matter that is moving has kinetic energy. The change from potential energy to kinetic energy doesn't happen all at once. The vase still has some potential energy until it hits the ground. Together, the potential energy and kinetic energy of the vase make up its **mechanical energy.**

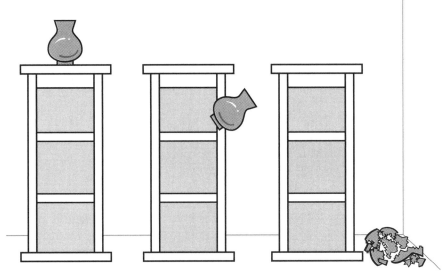

The vase has potential energy when it is on top of the shelf. As the vase falls, its potential energy becomes kinetic energy.

Kinetic energy is the energy that moving objects have.

An object's **mechanical energy** equals its kinetic energy plus its potential energy.

The higher an object is, the more potential energy the object has. For example, a rock at the top of a hill has more potential energy than the same rock at the bottom of the hill.

When the vase hits the ground, it makes a crashing sound. Sound is another form of energy. Sound travels through matter by making the matter *vibrate*, or move back and forth very quickly. These vibrations can travel through solids, liquids, and gases. When they travel to our ears, we hear sounds.

A boulder rolls down the side of a hill. Which three forms of energy does the boulder have or make as it is rolling down the hill?

  A potential energy, electricity, and heat

  B electricity, kinetic energy, and sound

  C electricity, heat, and chemical energy

  D potential energy, kinetic energy, and sound

The boulder is moving, so it must have kinetic energy. Choice A and choice C must be incorrect because they do not list kinetic energy. The boulder is not producing electricity, so choice B is incorrect. The boulder has potential energy because it is on a hill. It makes sound as it moves. The correct choice is D.

Energy Transfer and Change of Form

When you push a toy car, you are passing some energy to it so that it can move. When wind blows the curtains on an open window, energy from the wind passes to the curtains. When energy passes from one thing to another, it is called an **energy transfer.**

Not only does energy move from one thing to another, it can also change form. Picture a skateboarder at the top of a ramp. The skateboarder has potential energy. When she rolls down the ramp, she has kinetic energy because she is moving. When she is at the bottom of the ramp, she is moving fast. All her energy is kinetic. She does not have any more potential energy. The skateboarder's energy changed from one form to another.

Energy is changing forms all around us. When you turn on a lamp, electricity changes to light and heat. When you clap your hands, your body's mechanical energy produces sound. When you press a button to ring a doorbell, you complete a circuit. Electricity flows through the circuit and changes to sound.

The Flow of Energy

As energy moves from one thing to another in a system, it may change forms many times. When you turn on a flashlight, chemical energy in the battery changes to electricity. The electricity flows through the circuit to the light bulb. In the light bulb, electricity changes into light and heat.

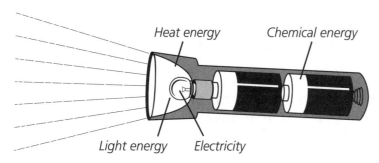

Heat energy   Chemical energy

Light energy   Electricity

In an ecosystem, energy changes form as it passes from the Sun through living things. Plants change light energy from the Sun into chemical energy in their bodies. When an animal eats a plant, the plant transfers chemical energy to the animal. In the animal's body, some of the chemical energy from the plant changes to heat. Much of the chemical energy changes to kinetic energy as the animal moves.

When people burn fossil fuels, they change chemical energy into other forms of energy. People commonly burn fossil fuels to produce electricity. In a power plant that burns fossil fuels, energy changes form many times.

> In an **energy transfer,** energy passes from one thing to another.
>
> *Transfer* can be a verb. It is something that energy does. It can also be a noun, as in the definition above.
>
> Forms of energy include
>
> chemical
> electrical
> light
> heat
> potential
> kinetic
> mechanical
> sound

132

It's Your Turn

Please read each question carefully. For each multiple-choice question, circle the letter of the correct response.

1 A cow eats some grass. What kind of energy does the grass transfer to the cow?

   A   chemical energy   **C**   kinetic energy

   B   electricity   **D**   light energy

2 A radio plays some music. In the radio,

   A   electricity is changing to light energy

   B   sound energy is changing to electricity

   C   electricity is changing to sound energy

   D   heat energy is changing to sound energy

3 In which situation does heat move from one object to another object because of friction?

   A   A candle burns itself out.

   B   A bucket of water freezes overnight.

   C   A person warms a pot of soup on the stovetop.

   D   A skateboarder drags her foot on the ground to slow down.

For this open-ended question, write your answers on the lines.

4 A student tries to make a circuit using a battery, two pieces of wire, and a light bulb. The picture below shows how he connected the materials.

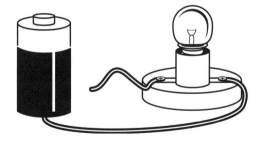

Will the bulb light up? Explain your answer.

_____

_____

Interactions of Energy and Matter

Major Understandings 4PS4.1d, g; 4PS4.2b

Energy can cause changes in matter. Some of these changes can be helpful. Others can be harmful. People use the helpful changes to make their lives easier.

How Energy Affects Matter

A puddle is made of liquid water, which is a kind of matter. Heat is a form of energy that is produced by the Sun. Heat from the Sun can warm the water in the puddle. The heat can make some of the water evaporate. **Evaporation** happens when matter changes from a liquid to a gas.

Electricity is another form of energy. When you turn on a light bulb, electricity flows through a thin wire in the bulb. The wire is made of metal. When the electricity flows through the wire, the wire heats up. It gets so hot that it glows. The electricity makes the wire give off light. Light is a form of energy.

Energy interacts with different kinds of matter in different ways. Some kinds of energy move through matter. For example, sound is a kind of energy. Sound energy can move only through matter. If there is no matter, sound energy cannot travel.

Sound energy travels by making matter **vibrate,** or move quickly back and forth. For example, imagine a drum. When you hit the top of the drum, the energy in your moving hand makes the top of the drum vibrate. The energy in the moving drum makes the air vibrate. The vibrations carry the sound energy through the air. Even the air inside your ears starts to vibrate.

The vibrating air moves tiny hairs in your ears. The hairs produce signals that travel to your brain. The signals tell your brain that you are hearing something. Your brain helps you recognize the sound.

The color of matter affects how it interacts with energy, such as heat and light. White objects tend to reflect heat and light. Black objects tend to absorb heat and light.

Evaporation is a change of matter from a liquid to a gas.

When an object **vibrates,** it moves back and forth very fast.

Sometimes you can see sound energy making matter move. The sound from a plane flying overhead can make water in a pond ripple. You can often feel the vibrations from loud sounds. Vibrations from very loud sounds can even move heavy objects.

A student wants to learn about how light affects matter with different colors. He paints four pieces of wood different colors.

A   B   C   D

The texture of an object also affects how it interacts with light. Smoother objects tend to reflect light. Rougher objects tend to absorb it.

The student places all four blocks in the sun. After 30 minutes, which will most likely feel coolest?

A block A

B block B

C block C

D block D

In general, light-colored objects reflect heat and light better than dark-colored objects. If an object reflects heat and light, it is less likely to warm up. So, the lightest block will be coolest. Choice A is correct.

Helpful and Harmful Interactions with Energy

Interactions between energy and matter can be helpful or harmful. For example, electricity is a very useful form of energy. People use electricity to run lights, heaters, and other devices. Most of the devices in your home use electricity. Some new kinds of cars even run on electricity.

Electricity can also be dangerous. Lightning is a form of electricity that can hurt or kill people. It can also start fires. Even the electricity in homes can be harmful if people do not use it carefully.

Electric sparks can start fires. Many fires in people's homes start when a spark touches paper or cloth. If electricity flows through a person's body, it can make the person's heart stop beating.

Which of these interactions between matter and energy is most likely to be *harmful* to people?

A Electricity makes a subway train move.

B Light energy from the Sun warms a building in the winter.

C Heat energy from lava makes trees burn.

D Kinetic energy in wind makes leaves fall off trees.

Moving subway trains are helpful to people. The Sun warming a building is also helpful to people. So, choices A and B are incorrect. Leaves falling off trees are usually not helpful or harmful. Choice D is incorrect. If heat from lava burns trees, the smoke could harm people. The fire could also move to people's homes. The correct answer is C.

Sound can also be helpful. The sound of an alarm or someone yelling can warn you of danger. Music can make you feel happy or relaxed.

However, very loud sounds can be harmful. The energy in loud sounds can damage a person's ears. Listening to loud music can make you lose your hearing. Being close to airplane engines can also harm people's ears. That is why many airport workers wear ear protectors that look like earmuffs.

The picture shows a toaster. Describe how matter and energy interact in a toaster. Describe <u>one</u> way these interactions can be helpful.

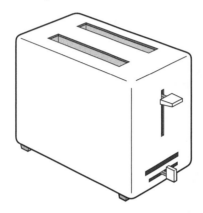

In a toaster, electricity moves through metal wires. The wires get hot. The heat toasts the bread. The interaction between the heat and the bread is helpful because it makes toast.

How Humans Use Interactions Between Matter and Energy

People use interactions between matter and energy in many ways. One important way is transportation. Cars, trucks, airplanes, trains, and ships use energy to move from place to place. Today, most of that energy comes from oil and gasoline. In older trains and ships, the energy came from coal. Oil, gasoline, and coal are fuels. A **fuel** is matter that gives off useful energy when it is burned.

Fuels contain chemical energy. When the fuels burn, the chemical energy changes into heat and kinetic energy. That energy interacts with matter. The interactions with matter can make objects move.

People use many other interactions between matter and energy. Remember that electricity runs many common devices. People also use interactions between sunlight and matter to heat their homes and make food.

A **fuel** is a substance that gives off energy when it burns.

It's Your Turn

Please read each question carefully. For each multiple-choice question, circle the letter of the correct response.

1 The drawing shows an electric circuit.

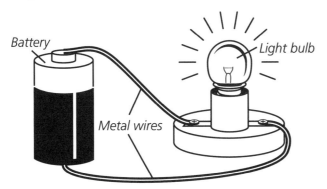

Which of these is an interaction between energy and matter that happens in this circuit?

A   Chemical energy in the battery makes the wire shorter.

B   Electricity from the battery makes the bulb give off light.

C   Heat from the bulb makes the battery stronger.

D   Kinetic energy in the wire makes the bulb absorb heat.

2 Sunlight can interact with matter in many ways. Which of these interactions is most likely helpful to people?

A   Skin can get burned if too much sunlight shines on it.

B   Sunlight can make buildings warmer in the summer.

C   Sunlight can kill germs in drinking water.

D   Looking straight at the Sun can make a person blind.

For this open-ended question, write your answers on the lines.

3 Identify <u>one</u> example of a device in your classroom that involves an interaction between electricity and matter. Describe the interaction between electricity and matter. Identify how people use the device.

_____

_____

_____

Forces and Motion

Major Understandings 4PS5.1a–f; 4PS5.2a, b

Motion is part of your everyday life. When you walk or run down the street, you are in motion. When you throw or kick a ball, you put the ball in motion. All motion starts, stops, or changes because of a force. Scientists study different kinds of motion in the world. They also study how forces affect the motion of objects.

Describing Motion

Objects in **motion** are changing **position.** This means they start in one location and end in another. When a bird flies from a tree to a rooftop, it is changing its position. The bird is in motion.

Scientists describe the motion of an object by comparing it to another object. The bird in the example above changed position compared to the tree. The runners below are changing position compared to the track.

Motion can seem different depending on how a person looks at it. For example, suppose you are sitting on a bench beside the road. Two of your friends pass by in a moving car. A scientist would say that both of your friends are moving compared to you. However, your friends are not moving compared to each other.

We can describe the position of an object using other objects, too. For example, you might say that a book is *on top of* a desk, *to the left of* a cup, or *under* a newspaper. If you push the book off the desk, you could describe the book's motion as falling from the desk to the floor.

Motion is a change in position.

The **position** of an object is its location.

To describe an object's position, you can use words such as *above, below, left, right, over,* and *under.*

Which of the following is the most accurate way to describe the position of a baseball?

A moving

B resting on top of third base

C falling down

D sitting on the left side

> To describe the position of an object, compare it to another object. Choices A, C, and D do not name another object to compare the baseball to. Therefore, choices A, C, and D are incorrect. Choice B describes where the baseball is compared to third base. The correct answer is B.

How Force Affects Motion

A **force** is a push or a pull. You know what it feels like to pull a door open or push a door shut. When you open or close a door, you are applying a force.

Forces can change the motion of an object. They can make an object move faster or slower. They can make an object move in a different direction. They can make an object start moving or stop moving. In general, a force can change the position of an object.

Most forces act between objects that are touching. A soccer ball moves when a player's foot pushes it. A door opens when you pull it. These are called **mechanical forces.** Simple machines are tools that can help you apply mechanical forces.

One type of simple machine is an inclined plane. An inclined plane is a ramp, a hill, or any sloped surface. You can push or pull objects along an inclined plane. An inclined plane makes it easier to move an object off the ground.

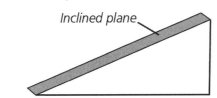

Inclined plane

An inclined plane is a sloped surface that makes work easier to do.

Another type of simple machine is a pulley. A pulley is a system with a rope and wheel. It can be used to lift objects. When you pull down on the rope, the object moves up.

A **force** is a push or a pull. A force can cause an object to speed up, slow down, or change direction.

Mechanical forces are forces that act between objects that are touching.

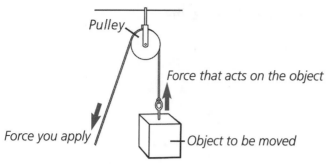

A pulley is a rope or string that passes around a wheel.

A lever is another simple machine. A lever is a stick that can move up or down around a point. A seesaw is a lever. If your friend sits on one end of a seesaw, you can push down on the other end and lift your friend into the air. Many common tools, such as crowbars and hammers, are also levers.

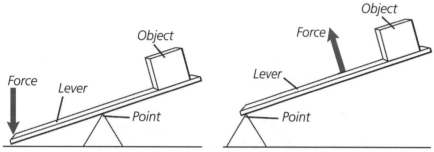

**A lever is a stick that helps you move an object.
Different levers move in different ways.**

Friction

A force that acts between objects or surfaces that are rubbing together is called **friction.** Friction acts against motion. That is, friction can make moving things slow down. When one surface moves past another, friction acts to slow down the movement.

When you kick a ball on the sidewalk, it might move very quickly. However, if the ball rolls into the grass, friction between the ball and the grass will cause the ball to slow down. The force of friction is greater for rough surfaces than for smooth surfaces. The force of friction between the ball and the grass is greater than the force of friction between the ball and the sidewalk. However, no matter how smooth a surface is, there is always some friction. Eventually, friction causes any object on Earth to stop moving.

Forces Acting at a Distance

Some forces act between objects that are not touching. For example, magnets attract metal with magnetic force. The magnet and metal do not have to touch for the force to act. The magnetic force, or **magnetism,** can attract or repel certain materials.

Friction is a force that acts between two objects or surfaces that are rubbing against each other. Friction acts against motion.

Magnetism is a force that magnets apply to other objects. A magnet will attract certain metals, like iron, nickel, and cobalt. A magnet may push away other materials, or it may have no effect on them.

Magnetic forces can act through solids, gases, and liquids. In the image below, the paper clip is inside a glass of water. When the magnet moves near the glass, the paper clip moves toward the magnet. The force of a magnet on an object gets smaller as the magnet moves away from the object. If the magnet in the image moves away from the paper clip, the magnetic force will get smaller, and the paper clip will fall to the bottom of the glass.

A student pulls a magnet away from the refrigerator and then lets it go. She notices that the magnet moves back to the refrigerator when it is 1 cm away, but it falls to the ground when it is 3 cm away. Explain why this happens.

The magnetic force between the magnet and the refrigerator gets smaller as the magnet moves away from the refrigerator. Eventually, the magnetic force is so weak that it does not attract the magnet. When this happens, the magnet falls to the ground.

All objects attract each other with a force called **gravity.** Gravity acts between objects that are not touching. Like the magnetic force, gravity acts through solids, gases, and liquids. This means that gravity will affect you when you are inside a building, flying through the air, or swimming underwater.

The force of gravity between most objects is very small. For example, the force of gravity between you and your desk is so small that you cannot feel it. However, the force of gravity between Earth and objects is very strong. Earth's gravity pulls all objects near Earth toward Earth's center. That is why a ball falls to the ground when you drop it.

Gravity is the force of attraction between two objects. Gravity is *always* a pull, never a push.

There is gravity between you and other people. However, you don't feel yourself being pulled toward the person sitting next to you. You are close together, but your masses are small. Compared with other forces, the force of gravity between you and the other person is weak, so you cannot feel it.

It's Your Turn

Please read each question carefully. For each multiple-choice question, circle the letter of the correct response.

1 **A student kicks a soccer ball. It flies into the air and then comes back down to the ground. The ball falls to the ground because**

  A the force of gravity pulled it back to Earth

  B it wanted to return to Earth's surface

  C it is heavy

  D the force of the wind pushed it down

2 **The picture shows a cat, a sidewalk, a tree, and some grass.**

Which of the following best describes the position of the cat?

  A on top of the grass   **C** to the left of the tree

  B to the west   **D** outside of the sidewalk

3 **A student holds a magnet over some pieces of iron. They move toward the magnet. When the student pulls the magnet away from the iron, the iron will probably**

  A fall off the table

  B be lifted off the table

  C move closer to the magnet

  D stop moving toward the magnet

4 A boy makes a pulley. He attaches a large basket to one end of the rope, and he pulls on the other end.

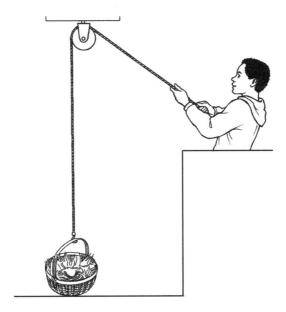

When the boy pulls on the rope, the basket will probably

  A become lighter

  B move upward

  C move downward

  D become magnetic

5 A student has two objects. Object A is a steel nail in a plastic container. Object B is a steel nail on the floor. What will most likely happen when she brings a magnet near the two objects?

  A Both objects will remain still.

  B Both objects will move toward the magnet.

  C Object A will move toward the magnet, but object B will remain still.

  D Object B will move toward the magnet, but object A will remain still.

For this open-ended question, write your answer on the line.

6 A girl is sledding down a snowy hill. At the bottom of the hill, the sled slows down and then stops. What force made the sled slow down and stop?

_____

143

Hands-On Lesson: Electricity and Magnetism

Major Understandings 4PS3.1e, f; 4PS4.1c; 4PS5.1e; 4PS5.2b

In this activity, you will study the electrical and magnetic properties of different materials. You will discover which materials do and do not let electricity pass through them. You will also discover which materials are and are not attracted to a magnet.

Materials

- electrical tester
- wooden toothpicks
- plastic toothpicks
- rubber band
- cotton string
- metal paper clip

- small iron nail
- new, shiny penny
- uninsulated copper wire
- new, shiny nickel
- 25 3-in.-x-5-in. index cards
- 2 bar magnets

Part I: Conducting Electricity

1 Your teacher will make the electrical tester for you to use. Make sure the electrical tester looks like the one shown in the drawing. You will use the tester to find out what materials are electrical conductors. An **electrical conductor** is a material that lets electricity pass through it easily.

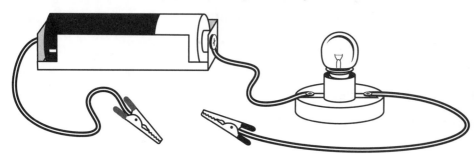

An **electrical conductor** is a material that conducts electricity easily, or allows electricity to pass through it easily.

2 Touch the two clips together to make sure the tester is working. Make sure to hold the clips by their handles. The bulb should light up. This means electricity has passed from the battery, through the bulb, and back to the battery. If the bulb does not light up, ask your teacher for help.

You may test materials not on the list. But check with your teacher before testing other materials.

3 Clip one wire to one end of the wooden toothpick. Clip the other wire to the opposite end of the toothpick. Does the bulb light up? If the bulb lights up, electricity has passed through the toothpick. Record your observation in the chart on the next page.

UNIT 4 The Physical Setting, Part 2

Object Tested	What happened to the light bulb?
wooden toothpick	
plastic toothpick	
rubber band	
string	
paper clip	
iron nail	
penny	
copper wire	
nickel	
index card	

4 Repeat step 3 with each of the other objects in the chart. When you are working with small objects, make sure that the clips do not touch each other.

Question 1: Which materials conducted electricity? Which did not? Fill in the chart below to describe your observations.

Conducts Electricity	Does Not Conduct Electricity

Part II: Exploring Magnetism

1 Place one end of a bar magnet against the wooden toothpick. Observe what happens when you move the magnet away from the toothpick.

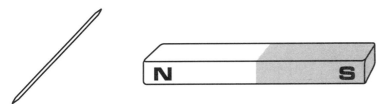

2 Use the chart below to record whether the magnet picks up the toothpick.

Object Tested	What happened when you brought the magnet near the object?
wooden toothpick	
plastic toothpick	
rubber band	
string	
paper clip	
iron nail	
penny	
copper wire	
nickel	
index card	

Materials made all or mostly of iron, nickel, or cobalt are attracted to a magnet. The U.S. coin called a *nickel* is not attracted to a magnet because it contains only 25% nickel. The rest is copper.

3 Repeat steps 1 and 2 with the other objects.

Question 2: Objects that stick to a magnet are *magnetic*. Which objects were magnetic? Which were not? Fill in the chart below to describe your observations.

Magnetic	Not Magnetic

4 Place an index card between a paper clip and the magnet as shown. Observe what happens. Record your observations in the table below.

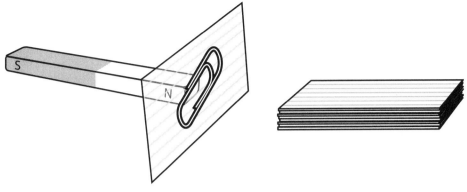

Number of Index Cards	Observations
1	
5	
10	
15	
20	
25	

5 Remove the index card from between the paper clip and the magnet. Stack five index cards together and put them between the magnet and the paper clip. Observe what happens and record your observations.

6 Repeat step 4 with 10, 15, 20, and 25 index cards.

Question 3: What happens as the number of index cards between the paper clip and the magnet increases?

_____

_____

Question 4: Based on your observations, make a conclusion about how the strength of the magnetic force is related to the distance between a magnet and a magnetic object.

_____

_____

7 Pick up both bar magnets. Lay down one bar magnet with its north pole (marked "N") facing to the right. Do not hold the magnet.

8 Move the south pole of the other magnet toward the north pole of the first magnet as shown below. Observe what happens.

Question 5: What happens when you move the north pole of one magnet toward the south pole of another magnet?

_____

9 Repeat step 8, but this time move the north pole of the second magnet toward the north pole of the first magnet.

Question 6: What happens when you move the north pole of one magnet toward the north pole of another magnet?

_____

Please read each question carefully. For each multiple-choice question, circle the letter of the correct response.

1 A scientist observes an object with only her senses. Which of the following observations does she most likely make about the object?

A   It has a mass of exactly 150 g.

B   It is red and hard.

C   It has a temperature of 30°C.

D   It is soft and magnetic.

2 A student tells her little brother that her lunchbox is made of matter. Her brother asks her how she knows. Which of these is the best answer?

A   "I can see it."

B   "It is very heavy."

C   "It has mass and takes up space."

D   "It takes up most of the space in my backpack."

3 Which of the following objects will most likely sink in water?

A   a metal necklace

B   a wooden bowl

C   a hollow plastic ball

D   a foam cup

4 A marble falls into a puddle of mud. Which of the following properties will most likely change?

A   volume

B   color

C   hardness

D   width

5 A student sorts six objects based on their properties. The groups are shown below.

Group A   Group B

Which of these objects would the student most likely place in group B?

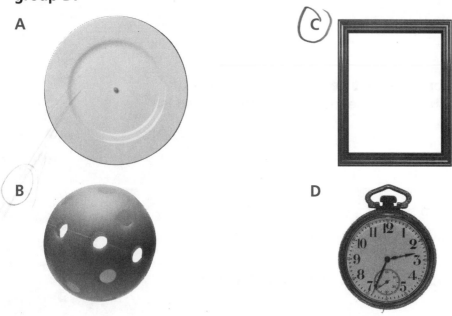

A

C

B

D

6 Which of these best describes how the state of water changes as temperature decreases?

A liquid water → ice → water vapor

B liquid water → water vapor → ice

C water vapor → ice → liquid water

D water vapor → liquid water → ice

7 A scientist drills a hole in a barrel of water. As water leaks out of the barrel, the scientist will most likely observe that the barrel changes in

A color

C weight

B shape

D hardness

8 A scientist is studying a substance with a fixed shape and volume. The scientist is most likely studying

A neon gas

B liquid gold

C oxygen gas

D solid carbon

9 A scientist puts a cold metal ball into a jar of warm water. Over time, the ball will

A shrink

B become warm

C make the water warmer

D fill the container

10 A student puts a battery in a flashlight and the bulb begins to glow. In this system,

A light in the battery becomes heat and electricity

B electricity in the battery becomes sound and kinetic energy

C chemical energy in the battery becomes electricity and light

D potential energy in the battery becomes chemical energy and light

11 The brakes on a bicycle work by rubbing on the edges of the wheels. Friction makes the wheels slow down. As the brakes rub on the wheels, the wheels most likely become

A stiffer

B thinner

C harder

D warmer

12 The picture below shows a pair of sunglasses.

What is the main reason people wear sunglasses?

A to absorb heat and stay warmer

B to protect them from sunlight

C to block the wind

D to reflect heat from the Sun

13 In which of these situations does chemical energy change to kinetic energy?

   A   A tree absorbs water through its roots.

   B   A fire warms the air in a room.

   C   Gasoline burning makes a car move.

   D   Electricity in a wire makes a radio work.

14 A student rolled a ball along the floor. After a while, the ball slowed down and stopped. Which of the following best explains why the ball did not keep rolling?

   A   No forces acted on the ball.

   B   The force of friction acted against the ball's motion.

   C   The force of gravity pushed the ball away from the floor.

   D   The ball was too heavy to keep moving.

15 The map below shows the positions of a house, a pond, and a playground.

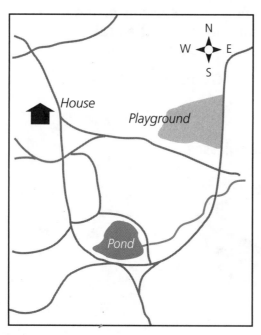

Which of these best describes the position of the house?

   A   east of the pond

   B   west of the playground

   C   south

   D   north

16 A student makes a lever to lift a large stone. The picture shows her lever.

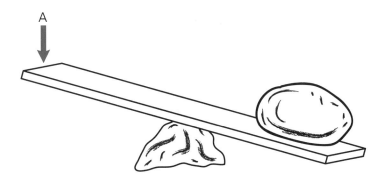

When the student pushes down on point A, the rock will most likely

A fall to the ground

B spin in place

C move upward

D break apart

17 A paper airplane is flying through the air. A strong gust of wind blows against the side of the airplane. The airplane will most likely

A change direction

B break apart

C become warmer

D shrink

18 A student drops a marble into a glass of water. Which of the following best explains why the marble sinks?

A The marble reacts with the water.

B Water pushes down on the marble.

C Gravity pulls down on the marble.

D The glass pulls the marble toward it.

19 Which of these objects will most likely conduct electricity?

A a rubber glove

B a paper airplane

C a plastic comb

D a steel screw

20 Gravity is a force that acts on things near Earth. Which of the following pictures shows the direction that gravity pulls objects?

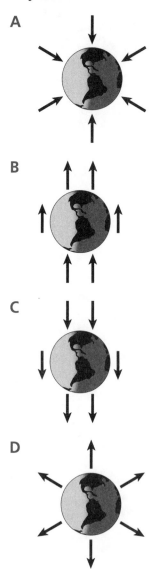

A

B

C

D

21 A scientist moves a wooden toothpick and a steel paper clip toward a magnet. What is most likely to happen?

A   The toothpick will stick to the magnet, but the paper clip will not.

B   Neither the paper clip nor the toothpick will stick to the magnet.

C   Both the toothpick and the paper clip will stick to the magnet.

D   The paper clip will stick to the magnet, but the toothpick will not.

For this open-ended question, draw your answer on the picture.

22 A student wants to make a circuit. She has a battery, a light bulb, and two pieces of wire. The picture below shows the battery and the light bulb.

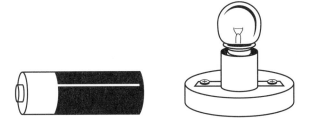

Draw lines on the picture to show how the student should connect the two wires to make the bulb light up.

For each open-ended question, write your answers on the lines.

23 The picture below shows a bear catching a fish.

List <u>two</u> forms of energy in the picture. Tell where each form of energy is found in the picture.

(1) _____

(2) _____

24 The picture shows a guitar being played.

Identify <u>one</u> way that energy and matter interact when a person plays a guitar.

_____

_____

25 A student holds a magnet 5 centimeters from an iron nail. The nail does not move toward the magnet. What should the student do to make the nail move toward the magnet?

_____

26 List <u>three</u> properties of a copper wire that a scientist can measure.

(1) _____

(2) _____

(3) _____

Unit 5
The Living Environment, Part 1

Earth is home to many different living things. In this unit, you will learn ways that living things are alike and different. You will also learn how living things interact. Finally, you will learn what can happen when their environments change.

There are six lessons in this unit:

1 **Living and Nonliving Things**   Living things are different from nonliving things. In this lesson, you will learn how living and nonliving things are similar and how they are different.

2 **Responding to the Environment**   The environment is always changing. To survive, living things must respond to those changes. In this lesson, you will learn how plants and animals respond to changes in the environment. You will also learn how they can cause changes.

3 **Life Cycles**   A living thing changes during its life. These changes make up its life cycle. Different living things change in different ways. In this lesson, you will learn about the life cycles of different plants and animals.

4 **Adaptations**   Plants and animals live in many different places. They have traits that help them survive in those places. In this lesson, you will learn why plants and animals that live in one place may look very different from those that live in another place.

5 **Inheritance**   Many living things look like their parents. This is because parents pass many of their traits to their offspring. In this lesson, you will learn what kinds of traits a living thing gets from its parents. You will also learn what kinds of traits a living thing acquires as it grows.

6 **Variation and Competition**   No two individuals in a group are the same. In this lesson, you will learn how these differences can make individuals more likely to survive and reproduce. You will also learn how groups of living things can change over time.

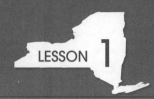
Living and Nonliving Things

Major Understandings 4LE1.1a–d; 4LE1.2a; 4LE3.1a, b; 4LE4.2a, b; 4LE5.1a

Scientists call all living things **organisms.** Organisms can look very different from one another. However, all organisms have certain characteristics. They all use food for energy. They all can grow. Every kind of living thing can reproduce to make more of its kind. Living things can also respond to their environment. For example, a sunflower can turn to face the Sun. A squirrel can go into a burrow to get out of the rain.

An **organism** is a living thing.

Characteristics of Living Things

All living things grow, or get bigger, during some part of their lives. Every kind of living thing can reproduce. Living things **reproduce** to make more of their kind. Like all living things, plants grow and change during their lives. Most plants grow from seeds. Under the right conditions, a young plant called a **seedling** will sprout from a seed.

When organisms **reproduce,** they make offspring that are like themselves.

Some animals grow from eggs. A fish grows from an egg to a fry to an adult. As it grows, it gets bigger and develops fins, scales, and other body parts.

A **seedling** is a young plant that grows from a seed.

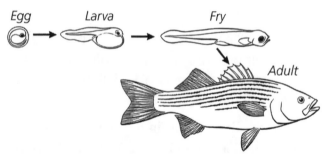

Egg   Larva   Fry   Adult

All plants and animals grow during their lives.

All plants and animals also need food. **Food** is anything that gives an organism energy. Plants and animals need energy to carry out their functions. For example, animals need energy to breathe and move. Plants need energy to grow and make seeds. Food also contains useful materials called **nutrients** that help organisms with growth and repair.

Food is any material used by an organism for energy, growth, or repair.

Nutrients are the useful materials in food.

All foods supply energy, but organisms cannot use all the energy in a food right away. They must first break down foods. In animals, the process of breaking down food is called **digestion.** Foods that are easy to digest give energy very quickly. Other foods take more time to digest but supply energy longer.

Animals break down food into nutrients in a process called **digestion.**

Getting energy is an important reason why organisms need food. However, organisms also use nutrients in food to help them grow and repair their bodies. For example, when you eat food, some of the nutrients in the food help your muscles and bones grow.

Why is a banana a food?

A It tastes good.

B It grows on trees.

C It supplies energy.

D It comes from a store.

To answer this question, think about the definition of a food. Choices A, B, and D are incorrect because the way something tastes, where it grows, and whether it comes from a store do not determine whether it is a food. The correct answer is C because foods supply energy.

If something enters an organism's body and is not used, it is not food. For example, if a dog swallows a plastic toy, the toy will pass through its body unchanged. The toy does not give the dog energy or materials to grow and repair its body. Therefore, the toy is not a food.

Although foods contain useful materials, they also contain materials that organisms cannot use. These materials are called **wastes.** For example, fruits and vegetables contain fiber. Many animals cannot use fiber for energy, growth, or repair. Fiber passes through their bodies and is eliminated. **Elimination** is the removal of waste materials from an organism.

Because plants make their own food, they produce fewer wastes than animals. Plants can store many of their wastes in special structures inside their cells. These structures prevent the wastes from harming the plant.

Plants and animals also need water to survive. They need water to help move materials inside their bodies. Most animals take in water through their mouths. Most plants take in water through their roots.

Materials in food that cannot be used become **wastes** in the organism's body.

Elimination is the process in which an organism gets rid of wastes.

All plants and animals need water.

Plants and animals need oxygen to live. They use oxygen to get energy from food. In the process, they make carbon dioxide waste. Animals get oxygen by breathing in air. Animals breathe out carbon dioxide before it harms their bodies. This process is called **respiration.**

Plants have tiny holes in their leaves that gases can move through. Carbon dioxide can move out of the plant through these tiny holes. Like animals, plants use oxygen to get energy from their food. Oxygen can move into the plant through the tiny holes in its leaves. Plants also produce some oxygen when they make food.

Structure and Function in Plants and Animals

Each plant and animal is a system. Like all systems, plants and animals are made up of different **structures,** or parts. An organism's body structures carry out different functions for the organism. A structure's **function** is the job it does. An organism's structures work together to help the organism get the things it needs.

Plants have structures called roots, stems, and leaves. Roots spread out under the soil to help plants take in water. Stems provide support for plants. They also carry water from the roots to the leaves. Leaves help plants take in gases and collect sunlight. Plants use water, air, and sunlight to make food in their leaves. The image of the pea plant below shows each of these structures.

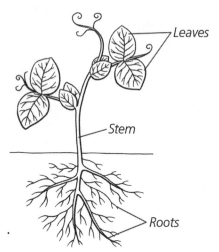

Each part of a pea plant has a certain function.

Deserts get very little rain. Many plants that live in the desert have long roots that spread out under the soil. Identify <u>one</u> way the roots of some desert plants can help them meet their needs.

Respiration is the exchange of gases between an animal and its environment. *Breathing* is another word for *respiration.*

An organism's **structures** are the parts that make up the organism's body.

The **function** of a structure is the job that it performs.

The roots of many plants also help to keep the plants in the ground. The roots grow under the soil and help hold the plants in place.

First, read the whole question to see if you can find any information. The question tells you that the desert doesn't get much rain. You should think about how long roots would help a plant get water in a very dry place. Long roots that spread out can help desert plants find and take in the small amounts of water in the soil.

Plants cannot make food when the Sun is not shining, so plants also store extra food in their bodies for later use. When plants make more food than they need, they can store the extra food in their roots and stems, or use the energy to produce fruits. Plants use the stored food for energy, growth, and repair when they are unable to make food.

Animals have structures that help them move. Animals need to move to find food and water. All animals can move from place to place at some point in their lives. They move around to find what they need to survive. Many animals that live on land, such as deer and birds, move using legs or wings. Other land animals, such as snakes, move by crawling on their bellies. Some animals that live in water swim using fins.

Animals have many different coverings on their bodies. Birds have feathers that keep them warm and help them fly. Fish and reptiles have hard scales that protect their skin. Many animals have fur that keeps them warm. A porcupine is covered in sharp spines. The spines protect the porcupine from other animals.

Both plants and animals have body parts for protection.

Animals also have special structures to help them with respiration. Most land animals use lungs for respiration. **Lungs** help an animal take in oxygen from air. People, wolves, reptiles, and birds have lungs.

Not all animals have lungs. Most animals that live in water use gills for respiration. **Gills** help animals take in oxygen from water. A few animals can take in and release gases through their skin.

When animals take in more food than they need, their bodies store the extra energy as fat. Body fat is a long-term store of energy. Many animals break down their fat stores when the supply of food is low. For example, bears and chipmunks sleep through the winter. They live off their body fat while they sleep.

Lungs are structures that help animals get oxygen from air.

Gills are structures that help an animal get oxygen from water.

Which animal structure has a function most similar to the function of the tiny holes in plant leaves?

A lungs   C stomach

B skeleton   D wings

First, think of the function of the tiny holes in leaves. The holes take in air. Look for an answer choice that has a similar function in animals. A skeleton does not take in air, so choice B is incorrect. A stomach helps an animal digest food, so choice C is incorrect. Wings help an animal move, so choice D is incorrect. Many animals use lungs to take in air, so the correct choice is A.

Characteristics of Nonliving Things

Nonliving things are not alive. Because they are not alive, nonliving things do not grow, take in nutrients, breathe, or reproduce. Nonliving things do not respond to their environments.

Sometimes it seems like a nonliving thing has characteristics of a living thing. For example, sometimes a river will get bigger when it rains. But a river does not breath or reproduce, so a river is not alive.

Some nonliving things are natural. A mountain is an example of a natural nonliving thing. Not all nonliving things are natural. Some nonliving things are made by humans. A computer is an example of a nonliving thing that is made by humans.

The insect in the picture below is sitting on a rock. Describe <u>two</u> reasons why the insect is considered a living thing. Describe <u>two</u> reasons why the rock is not considered a living thing.

The insect is a living thing because it can breathe, reproduce, grow, and take in nutrients. For example, the insect in the picture grasps its prey with its front legs. The rock does not have any of the characteristics of a living thing. For example, a rock does not grow, breathe, or reproduce.

It's Your Turn

Please read each question carefully. For each multiple-choice question, circle the letter of the correct response.

1 **What would most likely happen to an animal if it stopped eating food?**

   A It would die.

   B It would grow.

   C It would repair itself.

   D It would make its own energy.

2 **Which of the following statements correctly describes what plants and animals need to live?**

   A Animals need food, but plants do not.

   B Plants need water, but animals do not.

   C Animals and plants both need carbon dioxide.

   D Plants and animals both need oxygen.

3 **The picture shows a baby deer.**

This baby deer will grow a lot during its first year of life. What will most likely happen to its skeleton as it grows?

   A It will fall off.   **C** It will take in air.

   B It will get bigger.   **D** It will break down.

4 **Which of the following structures does not help a living thing keep warm?**

   A a bear's fur   **C** a dolphin's fins

   B a whale's fat   **D** a bird's feathers

Base your answers to questions 5, 6, and 7 on the pictures below and on your knowledge of science.

These pictures show two living things.

5 **What do these living things have in common?**

A   They both have roots.

B   They both move to find food.

C   They both reproduce.

D   They both take in air through leaves.

6 **What would most likely happen if the tree did not have roots?**

A   It would have too much oxygen.

B   It would not get enough air.

C   It would have too much food.

D   It would not get enough water.

7 **What happens to materials in food that the snail's body cannot use?**

A   They are eliminated.

B   They are stored as fat.

C   They help the snail grow.

D   They make the snail sick.

For this open-ended question, write your answers on the lines.

8 **Give <u>one</u> example of a naturally occurring nonliving thing. Give <u>one</u> way you know it is nonliving.**

_____

_____

Responding to the Environment

Major Understandings 4LE5.2a–g; 4LE6.1e

Environments change. They change from hour to hour. They change from day to day. They change from season to season. To survive, plants and animals must respond to those changes.

Plant Responses

Plants need sunlight to grow. They capture sunlight with their leaves. The more sunlight that falls on the leaves, the better the plants will grow. However, the Sun seems to move through the sky during the day. At different times of day, different amounts of sunlight shine on a plant.

Many plants respond to these changes by turning their leaves toward the Sun. They do this all through the day. Turning their leaves allows the plants to capture more sunlight.

A plant's leaves move very slowly. You cannot see them moving.

A student plants a seed in a flowerpot. He places the pot near a lamp.

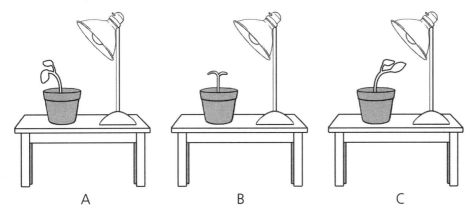

| A | B | C |

Which drawing shows how the plant will most likely grow?

A drawing A

B drawing B

C drawing C

First, notice that this question has only three answer choices. Most plants can move their leaves to face a light source. The plant will probably grow with its leaves facing the lamp. Drawing C shows the plant's leaves closest to the lamp. Therefore, the correct answer is C.

The amount of sunlight on a plant changes quickly. However, some environmental changes take longer. For example, the seasons change over many weeks. Plants respond to these changes in different ways. When the weather turns cooler, plants may lose their leaves and stop growing. When the weather turns warm again, the plants grow new leaves and flowers. They start growing again.

Plants must take in water to survive. When the environment does not supply enough water, plants may die. This happens during a drought. A **drought** is a long period during which an environment gets very little water from rain or snow. Some plants respond to droughts by growing more slowly. By growing slowly, they do not need as much water.

During a **drought,** much less rain or snow falls than is usual.

Animal Responses

Animals, including human beings, also respond to changes in their environments. Animals may change their behavior in response to changes. Or they may change what they look like.

Some environmental changes happen quickly. For example, when you walk out of a warm building into very cold air, your environment changes very quickly. If you are not dressed warmly enough, you will probably start shivering. Shivering helps you keep warm. However, if you walk out of a cold building into hot air, you do not start shivering. Instead, your body responds by sweating, or perspiring. Sweating helps to keep your body cool.

Dogs respond to hot weather by panting. Panting helps them cool off.

If something scares you, your heart beats faster. You also start to breathe faster. This gets you ready to run away from danger. If something is very scary, you may start to run away. Running away is another way animals respond to danger. Many animals respond to danger in this way.

Animals do not move only to get away from danger. They may also move from place to place to meet other needs. For example, animals in the desert may move from one place to another to find water.

Your body also changes in other ways when you are scared. Your eyes open wider. Your body makes a chemical called *adrenaline* that gives you energy. Your muscles get tighter. All of these changes help prepare you to run away or fight. Even if you do not run away, these changes still happen.

The cat in the picture below is responding to a change in its environment.

What kind of change is the cat probably responding to?

The cat's fur is sticking out, and its back is curved up. This makes the cat look larger. Many cats respond this way to a dangerous animal. By making itself look larger, the cat may scare away the dangerous animal.

Animals also respond to changes that take place over a long time. For example, animals respond in different ways to changes in the seasons. They may **migrate** as seasons change. Many kinds of birds migrate. Some kinds of insects and even some mammals also migrate.

Frogs, toads, chipmunks, bears, and other animals respond to the coming of cold weather in a different way. They hibernate. To **hibernate** is to go into a kind of long "sleep." The animal does not move very much. Its body's processes happen very slowly. So, the animal does not need to eat. Instead, it gets energy from fat stored in its body. When it wakes up in the spring, it has used up most of its fat. During the spring and summer, it eats a lot of food. It builds up more fat for the next winter.

Animals may also respond to long-term changes by changing what they look like. For example, arctic hares live in the far north. Foxes and other animals hunt the hares. To survive, hares must hide from their **predators.** Their fur changes color in the winter and in the summer. This color change helps them hide.

In the winter, snow covers the ground. Arctic hares have white fur in the winter. The white fur blends in with the snow. It helps the hare hide. In the summer, the snow melts. The ground is brown and gray. Arctic hares have brown or gray fur in the summer.

When an animal **migrates,** it moves from one ecosystem to another. Usually, animals migrate to avoid weather that is too hot, too cold, too dry, or too wet.

When an animal **hibernates,** its body's processes slow down. The animal seems to be asleep, but it does not wake up for many weeks or months.

A **predator** is an animal that eats other living things. It may hunt other animals or eat plants for food.

Winter

Summer

Arctic hares look different in winter than in summer. The change helps them survive.

A white-tailed deer begins to lose some of its fur. The fur that is left is thin. It also loses some of the fat underneath its skin. The deer is most likely responding to

  A an increase in rain in the area

  B a decrease in sunlight in the area

  C an increase in temperatures in the area

  D a decrease in predators in the area

Losing fur and fat will prevent the deer from becoming too warm. This change would help a deer survive an increase in temperatures. Therefore, the correct answer is C.

Animal Senses

Animals use their senses to detect changes in the environment. Most animals have the same five senses that people have: sight, hearing, touch, taste, and smell. Animals use their senses for many things. Senses can:

  • warn an animal of danger
  • help an animal find food, water, or shelter
  • help an animal find a mate

An animal's sense of sight can help it detect colors and changes in light. Its sense of hearing helps it detect sounds. Its sense of touch helps it detect textures, temperature, and size. Its sense of smell and taste help it detect the chemicals that give foods and other objects their smells and flavors.

Not all animals have all five senses. For example, some animals that live in very dark places are blind. Some animals also have senses that humans do not have. For example, some kinds of fish can sense magnetism.

Animals' senses can be different in other ways. For example, dogs can smell and hear things that people cannot. But people can see more colors than dogs can.

A student opens a container of food. She knows immediately that the food has spoiled, or gone bad. Which sense most likely warned the student that the food was bad?

A taste

B smell

C hearing

D touch

Spoiled food may taste bad or feel strange. However, the student knew the food was bad as soon as she opened the container. Therefore, she did not taste or touch the food. Choices A and D are incorrect. Spoiled food does not make different sounds than fresh food, so choice C is incorrect. Most foods begin to smell bad when they spoil. The student most likely smelled a bad odor from the food. The correct choice is B.

Why the Environment Changes

Living things cause some environmental changes. For example, beavers build dams on rivers and streams. The dams stop the water from flowing. The water floods the land.

Nonliving things also cause changes in the environment. For example, most winters in New York are cold. However, sometimes a winter is much warmer or colder than usual. Very warm or very cold weather can make it difficult for organisms to meet their needs.

Many living things rely on other living things for food. So, changes in the numbers of living things can affect other living things. For example, hawks and foxes eat mice. If a disease kills many mice, the hawks and foxes may not have enough food.

Owls eat snakes. Snakes eat frogs. Frogs eat flies. Which of these changes would most likely cause the number of snakes in an area to *decrease*?

A an increase in the number of flies

B an increase in the number of frogs

C a decrease in the number of owls

D a decrease in the number of flies

Make sure to read test questions carefully. If you think there is more than one right answer, reread the question. Try to identify information you missed the first time.

If the number of flies increases, more frogs will be able to find food and survive. If there are more frogs, more snakes will be able to find food and survive. If there are fewer owls, more snakes will survive. So, choices A, B, and C are incorrect. If there are fewer flies, fewer frogs will survive. If there are fewer frogs, fewer snakes will survive. Therefore, the correct choice is D.

It's Your Turn

Please read each question carefully. For each multiple-choice question, circle the letter of the correct response.

1 **A seed falls off a plant in the fall. The seed is buried in the soil. In the spring, the soil warms up. The seed will most likely respond by**

 A becoming smaller

 B moving to another place

 C sinking into the soil

 D sprouting roots and leaves

2 **Snakes eat mice. What probably happens when a mouse smells a snake?**

 A It breathes more quickly and runs away.

 B Its heartbeat slows down and it starts sweating.

 C It digs a larger burrow and hibernates.

 D Its muscles relax and it breathes more slowly.

3 **In the summer, gray whales swim to the Arctic Ocean, where they feed. In the winter, they swim south toward the equator, where they have their babies. This is an example of**

 A hibernation   C drought

 B migration   D growth

4 **Which characteristic most likely protects an animal from cold weather in the winter?**

 A shedding fur   C growing a thick layer of fat

 B changing color   D eating young plants

For this open-ended question, write your answers on the lines.

5 **Raccoons that live near people may eat rotten food from the people's trash. Identify <u>one</u> sense that raccoons probably use to find trash. Describe how that sense helps the raccoons find the trash.**

_____

_____

170 The Living Environment

Life Cycles

Major Understandings 4LE4.1a–g

All organisms begin life, grow and change, and then die. The time that passes between the beginning and the end of an organism's life is called its **life span.** Some organisms have life spans of only a few hours. Other organisms live for thousands of years. Many changes can take place during a life span. The changes can be very different for different living things.

Plant Life Cycles

During its life, a plant may go through many different stages. These stages make up the plant's **life cycle.** The picture below shows the life cycle of a flowering plant, such as a bean plant.

> A **life span** is the time between the beginning and end of the life of an organism.
>
> The **life cycle** of a plant or animal is the stages it goes through during its life.

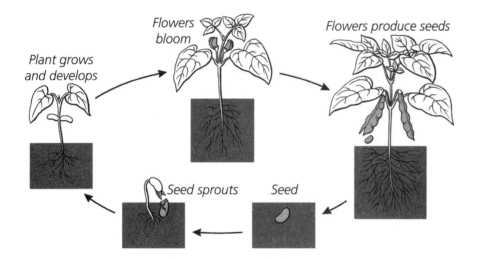

During the life cycle of a flowering plant, which of its parts produces seeds?

A roots

B leaves

C stems

D flowers

Roots anchor a plant. Stems hold it upright. Leaves make the plant's food. Flowers produce seeds. So, choice D is correct.

Animal Life Cycles

Animals also have life cycles. Animals change during their life cycles. Different animals change in different ways. Some animals look almost the same during their whole life cycle. The main difference between the adult and the young is that the adults are larger. Mammals, birds, fish, and reptiles all change in this way during their life cycles. Some insects also change in this way. The pictures below show two examples of animals that change in this way.

LIFE CYCLE OF A BIRD

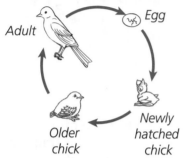

LIFE CYCLE OF A GRASSHOPPER

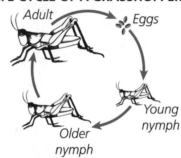

Baby birds hatch from eggs. Where do the eggs come from?

Adult birds lay eggs. The eggs hatch, and the chicks grow into adult birds. Those adult birds also lay eggs. In this way, the life cycle continues. This is true of all life cycles: in all life cycles, the adult organism produces young in some way.

Some animals have a different kind of life cycle. These animals change a lot during their lives. The young look very different from the adults. The pictures below show two examples of this kind of life cycle.

LIFE CYCLE OF A FROG

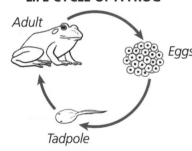

LIFE CYCLE OF A BUTTERFLY

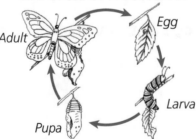

Scientists use special names to describe the different stages in a butterfly's life cycle. A butterfly starts its life as an egg. That is the first stage in its life cycle. The egg hatches into a **larva.** A butterfly larva is commonly called a *caterpillar.* The larva grows and eats a lot of food.

The eggs of different animals are different in size and form. Some are so small you would need a magnifier to see them. Some are larger than a dinner plate. Some eggs, like those of frogs, have soft coverings. Others, like those of birds, have hard shells.

The **larva** (plural, *larvae*) is the second stage in the life cycle of many insects.

UNIT 5 The Living Environment, Part 1

The third stage in the butterfly's life cycle is the **pupa.** When the larva finishes growing, it makes a hard shell around itself. The shell is called a *chrysalis*. The pupa develops inside the chrysalis. As it develops, the pupa slowly loses the parts of a larva. At the same time, it grows the parts of an adult butterfly. After a while, the adult butterfly breaks out of the chrysalis and unfolds its wings. The adult is the last stage in the life cycle. Adult insects lay eggs, starting a new life cycle.

The words *egg, larva, pupa,* and *adult* are also used to describe the stages of other insects' life cycles. For example, houseflies also lay eggs. The eggs hatch into larvae. The larvae form pupae. The pupae hatch into adults.

The pupa (plural, *pupae*) is the third stage in the life cycle of many insects.

The life cycle of a human is most similar to the life cycle of a

   A bird

   B housefly

   C salamander

   D butterfly

A human life cycle starts with a baby. The baby grows into a child. The child grows into an adult. Babies, children, and adults all look very similar. The main difference is size. Houseflies, salamanders, and butterflies all change form a lot during their life cycles. However, birds look about the same during their whole lives. Therefore, the correct answer is A.

Please read each question carefully. For each multiple-choice question, circle the letter of the correct response.

1 Which of these stages is part of the life cycle of every organism?

A eating plants

B growing

C hatching from an egg

D flowering

Base your answers to questions 2 and 3 on the pictures below and on your knowledge of science.

The pictures show four adult animals.

Bear

Bird

Lizard

Fly

2 Which animal changes form the most during its life cycle?

A fly

B bear

C bird

D lizard

3 Which of these best describes the life span of an organism?

A A robin lays an egg.

B A seed grows into a seedling.

C A sea turtle hatches from an egg, grows, and then lays more eggs.

D A plant sprouts from a seed, grows, and then dies.

For this open-ended question, write your answers on the lines.

4 Describe <u>two</u> stages in the life cycle of a radish plant.

(1) _____

(2) _____

Adaptations

Major Understandings 4LE3.1a–c; 4LE5.1b; 4LE6.1f

Different environments are homes to different kinds of organisms. An *environment* is everything that is around an organism. It includes living things, such as plants and animals, and nonliving things, such as rocks and water.

A feature of an organism that helps it survive and reproduce is called an **adaptation.** Some adaptations are part of a plant's or animal's body. Others are behaviors, or ways a plant or animal acts. Plants and animals in different environments need different adaptations to help them survive.

Animal Adaptations

Most animals that live in wet areas have adaptations that help them swim or get things from the water that they need to survive. Beavers build their homes on rivers. A beaver has sharp teeth and strong jaws that let it cut down wood for shelter and food. It also has a large, flat tail. When the beaver is in danger, it slaps the tail on the water. It makes a loud sound. It warns other beavers of the danger.

Fish, such as the brook trout, live underwater. A brook trout has gills. Gills are organs that allow an animal to get oxygen from water. A brook trout's tail, fins, and smooth scales allow it to move easily through water. This helps it to find shelter, eat food, and escape from predators.

Many animals on land have legs that help them move around. Most land animals, including humans, have eyes, noses, ears, tongues, and skin to help them sense the environment.

Some animals have adaptations to help them stand out. In many cases, bright colors and patterns are warnings that an animal is poisonous or venomous. Monarch butterflies are brightly colored and poisonous for birds to eat. Eastern coral snakes have brightly colored bands that signal that they are venomous. In other cases, an animal uses its colors to attract a mate. For example, peacocks show their colorful **plumage** to a female when they want to attract her.

Some animals have adaptations that help them blend in with the environment. This is called **camouflage.** Blending in can help an animal hide from predators. Blending in can also help a predator sneak up on its **prey.**

> An **adaptation** is a characteristic of an organism that helps it survive in its environment.
>
> The brook trout is the state fish of New York.
>
> **Plumage** is the color and pattern of a bird's feathers.
>
> **Camouflage** is a color or design that allows an animal to blend in with its environment.
>
> An animal's **prey** are the organisms the animal eats.

Predators have a hard time seeing this walking stick insect. Looking like a stick is an adaptation that helps the insect survive.

Hiding is not the only way animals protect themselves. Some animals use sharp claws and teeth to protect themselves. Some animals, such as skunks, spray a liquid with a very bad smell. The liquid smells so bad that it scares away predators. Some animals have thick, hard coverings on their skin. For example, a turtle's shell helps to protect it from predators.

The picture shows a baby deer.

Many young animals have extra camouflage to help them blend in with their environments. Young animals are often too small and slow to fight or run away from predators. The extra camouflage helps them hide.

The baby deer is mostly brown, with white spots. Explain how this color pattern is an adaptation.

An adaptation helps an organism survive. Baby deer are small and weak. They cannot run away from danger very quickly. Their color patterns are camouflage. The white spots on the baby deer's brown fur look like spots of light on the ground. The spots make the baby deer blend in with its environment. The camouflage makes it harder for predators to see the baby deer.

Plant Adaptations

Plants also have adaptations. The shape and size of a plant's leaves are adaptations to the environment. Plants lose water through their leaves. If a plant lives in a dry environment, it must conserve water. Most plants that live in deserts have very small or narrow leaves. Small leaves lose less water than large leaves do.

A plant's leaves are adapted to its environment.

The spines on a cactus are actually its leaves. The small, narrow spines do not lose water very quickly. Many cactuses have thick stems. The stems have a waxy outer layer. The stems store water and food for the cactus.

Plants also have adaptations that keep animals from eating them. Some plants have leaves that smell or feel bad to a predator. Other plants make chemicals that can make predators sick. These adaptations keep predators from eating the plant.

Plants use sunlight to make food. They absorb sunlight through their leaves. Some plant adaptations help the plant get more sunlight. For example, some vines wrap around tree trunks. The higher they climb up the trunk, the more sunlight they get. Climbing the trunk takes less energy than building a strong trunk of their own. So, climbing the trunk of a tree is an adaptation.

The size of a plant's roots is an adaptation. The roots of a plant help it take in water and nutrients from soil. Plants such as the mesquite tree grow in dry environments. In a dry environment, water is found only deep in the soil. Mesquite trees have long roots that reach deep underground to take in water.

Many plants grow from seeds. A young plant is more likely to survive if it grows far from its parent plant. If the young plant grows too close to the parent, the parent may block sunlight or water from getting to the young plant. Therefore, for a seed to grow, it must move far from its parent plant. However, seeds cannot move on their own.

Plants rely on the environment to carry their seeds away. For example, dandelion seeds are very small and light. They have a fluffy sail. The wind catches the sail and carries the seed away. The sail is an adaptation that helps the plant survive. Water can also carry some plant seeds away.

Plants also rely on animals to carry their seeds. Some plants make delicious fruits. When an animal eats the fruit, it also eats the seeds. The animal does not digest the seed. The seed passes out of the animal's body. By that time, the animal has moved far from the plant.

This picture shows the seed of a cocklebur plant.

How do the spines on the cocklebur seed help the seed move away from its parent plant?

    A They stop animals from eating the seed.

    B They stick to an animal's fur.

    C They hold the seed onto the plant's stem.

    D They help the seed dig into the ground.

> If no animals ate the seeds, the seeds would not be carried away. Choice A is incorrect. If the seed does not fall off the plant, it cannot grow into a new plant. Choice C is incorrect. If the seed dug into the ground, it would be less likely to move away. Choice D is incorrect. The spines on the seed help it stick to an animal's fur. The animal carries the seed far from the parent plant. Therefore, the correct answer is B.

Changing Environments

Some environments change a lot during a year. For example, in New York, the winters are cold and the summers are hot. Animals that live in these environments have adaptations that help them adjust to different seasons. Before winter, black bears eat a lot of food. This helps them store body fat, which they use for energy during the winter hibernation. In the summer, a cat sheds its fur. This helps it to stay cool when it is hot outside.

Adaptations for one environment may not be helpful in another environment. For example, arctic foxes live in cold, snowy places. They have thick, white fur. Their fur keeps them warm. It also helps them blend in with the snow. If an arctic fox's environment became warmer, it might not survive. Its fur would make it too hot. If the snow melted, the fox would no longer blend in. Its predators would be able to see it more easily. It would not be able to sneak up on its prey. It might die.

If environmental changes are bad enough, many organisms may die off. In some cases, all of the members of a species die. When this happens, the species is *extinct*.

It's Your Turn

Please read each question carefully. For each multiple-choice question, circle the letter of the correct response.

1 **A bird eats mainly large, heavy seeds. The seeds have a thick shell. The bird has to break the shell with its beak before it can eat the seeds. Which of these pictures most likely shows the bird?**

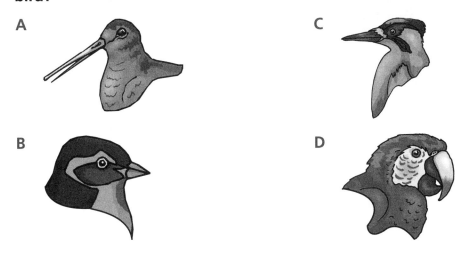

A

C

B

D

2 **Poison-arrow frogs have very bright colors. The skin of a poison-arrow frog contains deadly poisons. Which statement best explains how the adaptation of brightly colored skin is helpful to the frog?**

A   It lets the frog sneak up on prey.

B   It warns predators not to eat the frog.

C   It makes the frog look like a harmless animal.

D   It helps the frog blend in with the environment.

3 **The picture shows a bee cleaning its proboscis. A proboscis is a long, tongue-like organ.**

Which of these describes a way that the bee's proboscis helps it survive in its environment?

A   Its shape helps the bee fly.

B   Its color helps the bee hide from predators.

C   Its length helps the bee get food from flowers.

D   Its motion helps the bee keep cool on hot days.

4 **The picture shows the leaves of a plant.**

This plant most likely lives in an environment that is

A   hot and dry

C   warm and rainy

B   cold and windy

D   cold and dry

For this open-ended question, write your answers on the lines.

5 **Suppose a rain forest suddenly became very dry. Describe <u>one</u> thing that would probably happen to the plants in the rain forest. Explain your answer.**

_____

_____

Inheritance

Major Understandings 4LE2.1a, b; 4LE2.2a, b

Most living things look and act a lot like their parents. For example, puppies look and act a lot like adult dogs. Scientists say that they have similar *traits,* or features. Some traits are part of an organism's body. They make up how the organism looks. These are called *physical traits.* Other traits are not part of an organism's body. They make up the way the organism acts.

Inherited Traits

Inherited traits are traits that parents pass to their offspring. They are traits that a living thing is born with. If the environment changes, most inherited traits do not change.

A single living thing is called an **individual.** Most individuals look like their parents. This is because when parents reproduce, they transfer many traits to their offspring. For example, a girl may have blue eyes like her mother. Most tall people have tall parents. A puppy has four feet, like its parents do. Eye color, height, and number of feet are inherited traits.

Parents pass on **inherited traits** to their offspring.

You cannot see all inherited traits easily. Some inherited traits affect how an organism looks on the inside.

An **individual** is a single living thing.

When puppies are born, they look like their parents.

Plants also inherit traits from their parents. For example, most plants have the same shape of leaves as their parents. The shape of a plant's leaves is an example of an inherited trait.

A **species** is a group of organisms that are very similar to each other. For example, all lions are members of the same species. Individuals from the same species look like each other because they share many of the same traits. Individual lions look a lot like their parents, but they also look like all of the other lions in the world.

A **species** is made up of organisms that are all very similar to one another.

Individuals can also inherit behaviors from their parents. An inherited behavior is called an **instinct.** Instincts are behaviors that organisms are born knowing how to do. For example, many birds build nests. They do not have to learn how to build nests. They are born knowing how to do it. Nest building is an instinct.

Instincts help individuals survive. For example, ducklings have an instinct to stay near their mother after they hatch. Young ducklings are safer near their mother. Their instincts help them stay safe.

Ducklings do not need to learn to follow their mother. Following their mother is an instinct. This instinct helps the ducklings stay safe.

Why does a young giraffe have a long neck?

  A It inherited instincts from its mother.

  B It developed a long neck from stretching.

  C It learned to grow its neck to reach food.

  D It inherited some physical traits from its mother.

> The question is asking you about a physical trait of a young animal. Choices A and C do not describe physical traits. Choice B does not describe an inherited trait. A giraffe is born with a long neck. It does not get one from stretching. Therefore, choices A, B, and C are incorrect. The correct choice is D.

Acquired Traits

Some traits are not inherited. An individual is not born with them. Instead, the organism gets them over time. These traits are called **acquired traits.** Acquired traits can change as the environment changes.

An **acquired trait** is a trait that an organism develops during its lifetime.

UNIT 5 The Living Environment, Part 1

Some acquired traits affect part of an organism's body. For example, a person may have a scar or short hair. However, that person's child will not be born with a scar and short hair.

Both plants and animals can have acquired traits. The picture below shows an example of an acquired trait in a plant.

The damaged leaf did not inherit this trait from its parents. The insect damage is an acquired trait.

Some behaviors are acquired. Behaviors that are acquired are called **learned behaviors.** Many animals learn different behaviors as they interact with their environment. For example, young lions learn to hunt by watching their mother hunt. Dogs can learn to do tricks, such as playing dead and rolling over. A child can learn to read and speak. Lions, dogs, and children are not born knowing how to do these things. They learn these behaviors as they grow.

A **learned behavior** is something an organism is not born knowing how to do.

The picture below shows a deer.

Identify <u>one</u> trait this deer will probably pass on to its offspring. Identify <u>one</u> trait this deer will probably not pass on to its offspring.

Only inherited traits can be passed on to offspring. The deer's color, height, number of legs, and body shape are inherited traits. It will probably pass them on to its offspring. The deer's broken antler is an acquired trait. It will not pass this trait on to its offspring.

It's Your Turn

Please read each question carefully. For each multiple-choice question, circle the letter of the correct response.

Base your answers to questions 1 and 2 on the information below and on your knowledge of science.

Different kinds of plants have different traits. Some plants, such as pine trees and oak trees, have hard, woody stems. Other plants, such as grasses and sunflowers, have soft, fleshy stems. Pine trees have sharp, needlelike leaves. Oak trees, grasses, and sunflowers have soft green leaves.

1 Which of these traits would the offspring of a pine tree most likely have?

   A woody stem, soft green leaves

   B fleshy stem, needlelike leaves

   C woody stem, needlelike leaves

   D fleshy stem, soft green leaves

2 This paragraph describes

   A instincts   **C** inherited physical traits

   B learned behaviors   **D** acquired physical traits

3 Which of the following is an example of a learned behavior?

   A a child growing taller

   B a robin building a nest

   C a parrot repeating words

   D a bear hibernating through winter

For this open-ended question, write your answers on the lines.

4 A child has black hair, brown eyes, a scar on her chin, and pierced ears. Identify <u>one</u> of these traits that the child probably inherited from her parents. Identify <u>one</u> of these traits that the child probably did not inherit from her parents.

A trait the child probably inherited is _____.

A trait the child probably did not inherit is _____.

Variation and Competition

Major Understandings 4LE3.2a, b; 4LE5.1b; 4LE5.2g; 4LE6.1f

Remember that a species is a group of organisms that are all very similar. The members of a species have many traits in common. However, they also have some differences. For example, you do not look exactly like your parents. You and your parents are members of the same species: humans. But you each have some traits that make you different from each other. Every living thing has some traits that make it different from other members of its species. These differences are called **variations.**

A **variation** is a difference between two organisms that are part of the same species.

These kittens have variations that make them different from each other.

Individual Variations

An organism's traits can affect its ability to survive and reproduce. For example, all hawks have broad wings, very good eyesight, and hooked beaks. These traits help them fly, see their prey, and kill their prey. However, individual hawks can have variations that help them survive better than other hawks.

For example, one hawk may have better vision than another hawk. This variation might help the first hawk catch more food. If it can catch more food, it is more likely to survive. Hawks that live longer have more offspring. They may pass on their good vision to their offspring. Their offspring will also be more likely to survive.

Rabbits are food for hawks. Individual rabbits that have better hearing than other rabbits also have a better chance of surviving and reproducing. They can hear a hawk's approach sooner and escape to safety. Rabbits that survive longer have more offspring. They may pass on their good hearing to their offspring. Their offspring will also be more likely to survive.

Some variations can help an individual attract more mates than another. For example, many male birds have colorful feathers to attract females during mating season. Peacocks have long and showy tail feathers. They fan out these feathers to attract females. A peacock with longer or brighter tail feathers will attract more mates than other peacocks.

Organisms that attract mates easily will reproduce more often. That is, they will have more offspring. When peacocks with long tail feathers reproduce, they could pass the long-tail trait on to their offspring. Because they have this trait, the offspring will probably also attract mates easily.

Name <u>one</u> trait that would probably help an individual mouse survive.

Many different animals hunt mice. Traits that help a mouse avoid its predators will help it survive. Some traits that would help a mouse avoid predators are camouflage, good hearing, and a good sense of smell.

Competition

Living things need resources such as water, food, light, and space. They get these resources from the environment. When resources are limited, living things in an environment may compete. **Competition** is the struggle between organisms for the same resource.

For example, plants compete for light and space. In a forest, oak trees grow tall. Their broad leaves block sunlight from shorter plants. When a large tree, such as an oak, falls in a forest, sunlight can reach the ground. This allows new plants to grow.

Different kinds of animals may compete for the same food in an environment. For example, squirrels, blue jays, and deer gather or eat acorns in the autumn. The animals compete for acorns, especially when there are not many acorns. Animals that do not find enough acorns to eat may not survive.

Competition can also happen between members of the same species. Animals of the same species may compete for food or a place to live. They may also compete for mates. For example, male white-tailed deer grow antlers during mating season. They use their antlers to fight with other males. Stronger males with bigger antlers will win more mates.

Offspring that inherit traits that help them survive and reproduce are likely to pass those traits to their own offspring. If peacocks with longer tails reproduce more often, then over time more peacocks will have long tails.

Competition happens when organisms struggle for the same resource.

Living things need resources to meet their basic needs. If an organism cannot compete well for resources, it may not survive.

What is the most likely reason an eagle and a hawk would compete?

A They eat the same food.

B They have the same mates.

C They are both types of birds.

D They have too many resources.

To answer this question, think about why organisms compete. Choice D is incorrect because having too many resources does not lead to competition. An eagle and a hawk are different species, so they do not have the same mates. Therefore, choice B is incorrect. Choice C is incorrect because many birds do not compete with each other. The correct choice is A. When organisms eat the same food, they may compete with each other.

Changing Environments

An organism's traits can help it survive if the environment changes. For example, suppose a species of mouse lives in a forest. The mice are mainly brown. Some are lighter brown, and some are darker brown. Their color helps them blend in with the dead leaves and soil on the ground in the forest.

Imagine that the environment starts to change. There is less rain. The trees in the forest cannot get enough water. They start to die. Eventually, the forest floor is covered in grass. The grass turns light brown from lack of water. As the grass dies, the forest floor is covered in light brown grass.

The mice that are darker brown will not blend in with the dead grass very well. Predators will be more likely to see and catch them. More light brown mice will survive. Over time, there will be more and more light brown mice.

An organism's different offspring are not equally likely to survive and reproduce. Individual variations make certain offspring more likely to survive in their environment. If the environment changes, their brothers or sisters may be more likely to survive.

Suppose an area begins to get colder. A bird with which of these variations would be most likely to survive?

A brighter colors than other birds

B better eyesight than other birds

C thicker feathers than other birds

D a sharper beak than other birds

The bird will die if it cannot stay warm as the environment gets colder. Brighter colors, better eyesight, and a sharper beak would not help the bird stay warm. Thicker feathers would keep the bird warmer. The correct answer is C.

It's Your Turn

Please read each question carefully. For each multiple-choice question, circle the letter of the correct response.

1 **Rabbits that live in the Arctic have thicker fur than rabbits that live in the desert. How is thick fur an advantage for a rabbit in the Arctic?**

   A   It helps the rabbit stay cool.

   B   It helps the rabbit find a mate.

   C   It helps the rabbit survive in the cold.

   D   It helps the rabbit escape from hawks.

2 **Which of these variations would probably help a plant survive if the environment gets drier?**

   A   larger leaves

   B   longer roots

   C   brighter flowers

   D   smaller seeds

3 **A student puts three different fish in an aquarium. Which of the following would most likely lead to competition among the fish?**

   A   limited space

   B   plenty of mates

   C   high food supply

   D   the presence of plants

For this open-ended question, write your answer on the lines.

4 **River otters, such as the one in this picture, are mammals that live on land and in water. They mainly eat fish.**

   Name <u>two</u> traits that could make one otter more likely than another otter to catch fish.

   (1) _____

   (2) _____

Please read each question carefully. For each multiple-choice question, circle the letter of the correct response.

1 The picture shows a crab.

The crab's shell is an adaptation that

A   helps the crab find food

B   helps the crab swim

C   allows the crab to reproduce

D   protects the crab from predators

2 Most plants that grow underwater can absorb water directly into their leaves. Because of this adaptation, they do *not* need

A   stems

B   flowers

C   roots

D   seeds

3 Beavers make their shelter from trees that they cut down. They use their teeth to cut through the tree trunks. Which of the following traits would most likely help an individual beaver get food?

A   strong jaws

B   a flat tail

C   good eyesight

D   waterproof fur

4 Male white-tailed deer use their antlers to fight each other for mates. Which of the male white-tailed deer shown below will probably have the most mates?

A

B

C

D

5 Which of the following is an example of competition?

A Two different foxes hunt a vole.

B A bobcat chases a hare for food.

C A bird picks insects off a rhinoceros.

D A tick lives on a dog's skin.

6 Penguins live in cold environments. They have thick layers of fat and feathers to keep their bodies warm. What would most likely happen to a penguin if it were put in a desert?

A It would get too hot and die.

B It would get used to the heat.

C It would find a cold spot to live in.

D It would move back to a cold area.

7 A person walks outside on a cold day. The person is not wearing a jacket. The person will most likely

A start to sweat

B start to shiver

C feel hungrier

D grow thicker hair

8 **Which of these senses could help a cat sense the warmth from a fire?**

A   sight

B   taste

C   smell

D   touch

9 **This caterpillar is eating a leaf.**

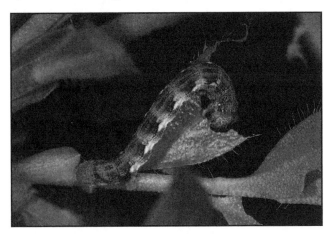

When the caterpillar has eaten the whole leaf, it will probably

A   die

B   reproduce

C   get smaller

D   move to a new place

10 **Which of these steps is not part of the life cycle of a bluebird?**

A   hatching from an egg

B   developing into a pupa

C   laying eggs

D   dying

11 **A grass's life span begins when a grass seed starts to grow. The end of the grass's life span happens when the grass**

A   dies

B   grows taller

C   reproduces

D   forms roots

Note that this question has only three answer choices.

12 **A housefly larva will next become**

   A   an egg

   B   a pupa

   C   an adult

13 **An acorn is the seed of an oak tree. A squirrel buries an acorn in the ground. What will the acorn most likely look like in two years?**

A   **C**

B   **D**

14 **A student is studying three insects: grasshoppers, moths, and ants. What will the student most likely learn about their life spans?**

   A   All insects live for about 70 years.

   B   Most insects have a longer life span than humans.

   C   Different insects have different life spans.

   D   Most insects live for only a few hours.

15 **A young plant will probably inherit which trait from its parents?**

   A   torn leaves   **C**   a broken branch

   B   rough bark   **D**   a bird's nest

Base your answers to questions 16 and 17 on the information below and on your knowledge of science.

A student places a seed in a container of soil. He puts the container with the seed in a well-lit room. The student waters the seed every day. After one week, the student observes a stem with two small green leaves pushing its way out of the soil.

16 If the student stops watering the plant, it will probably

  A   get taller every day

  B   become unhealthy and then die

  C   stay healthy but not grow

  D   turn back into a seed

17 How will the student be able to tell that the plant is growing?

  A   It will stay green.

  B   Its leaves will fall off.

  C   It will get bigger.

  D   Its roots will get shorter.

Base your answers to questions 18 and 19 on the pictures below and on your knowledge of science.

The pictures show four animals.

Bear

Mouse

Fish

Turtle

18 All of these animals

  A   get rid of wastes   C   breathe air

  B   lay eggs   D   eat fruit

19 The fish is different from the other animals because it

  A   eats   C   gets oxygen from water

  B   reproduces   D   eliminates wastes

20 Which of these traits would a boy most likely inherit from his parents?

A ability to play the trumpet

B brown eyes

C short hair

D ability to speak two languages

21 Which of these best explains why dogs and cats look different?

A They are members of different species.

B They inherit some traits from each other.

C They compete for food.

D They need different kinds of shelter.

For each open-ended question, write your answers in the tables.

22 The pictures show four objects.

| Rock | Bear | Frog | Book |

Fill in the table below to show which objects are alive and which objects are not.

Alive	Not Alive

23 **The pictures show four objects.**

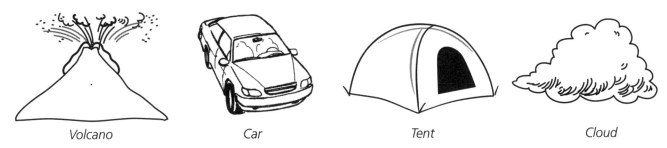

Volcano   Car   Tent   Cloud

Fill in the table below to show which objects are human-made and which objects are natural.

Human-Made	Natural

For each open-ended question, write your answers on the lines.

24 **Name __two__ things all animals need to survive.**

(1) _____

(2) _____

25 **The picture shows a desert.**

Identify __two__ characteristics of the desert that an organism would have to be adapted to.

(1) _____

(2) _____

26 If a snake does not eat, it will die. Identify <u>two</u> reasons the snake needs to eat in order to survive.

(1) _____

(2) _____

27 The weather in New York gets cold in the winter. Describe <u>two</u> ways some animals respond to cold weather. One way should be a behavior. The other way should be a change in the animal's body.

(1) _____

(2) _____

28 The picture shows a maple tree in summer.

Describe <u>one</u> way the maple tree will respond when summer changes to fall.

_____

29 The picture shows a hummingbird getting food from a flower.

Describe <u>one</u> adaptation that probably helps the hummingbird get food from the flower.

_____

Unit 6
The Living Environment, Part 2

Living things need food, water, and other things to survive. They meet their needs by interacting with each other and the environment. People depend on the environment to meet many of their needs. In this lesson, you will learn how people and other living things interact to meet their needs. You will also learn how human actions affect the environment.

There are three lessons in this unit:

1 **Food Chains**   All the living and nonliving things in an area make up the parts of an ecosystem. The living things there play various roles. In this lesson, you will learn about those roles. You will also learn how the living parts of an ecosystem meet their needs for food.

2 **Human Needs**   All living things have needs. In this lesson, you will learn what humans need to survive, such as healthy food, clean water, and exercise. You will also learn how humans meet their needs.

3 **Humans and the Environment**   Humans affect the environment in many ways. Some ways that humans affect the environment are harmful. We also do things that help the environment. In this lesson, you will learn how human actions help and harm the environment. You will also learn how we can reduce the negative effects of our actions.

Food Chains

Major Understandings 4LE6.1a–d; 4LE6.2a, b

Each of the living things in an ecosystem has a different role. Some living things are producers. Some are consumers. Producers use energy from the Sun to make their own food. This energy is transferred to consumers when the plants are eaten. Consumers can also transfer energy to other consumers.

The Roles of Organisms in Ecosystems

Plants and other living things that use air, water, and energy from sunlight to make their own food are called **producers.** Producers are very important in ecosystems. Without producers, none of the other living things in an ecosystem would have food.

Remember that animals cannot make their own food. Instead, animals get food by eating other living things. Organisms that *consume,* or eat, other organisms are called **consumers.** All animals are consumers.

Identify <u>one</u> organism in the picture below that is a producer and <u>one</u> organism that is a consumer. Explain your answer.

Producers are organisms that use energy from sunlight to make their own food.

Consumers are organisms that eat other organisms for food.

All organisms are either producers or consumers. You might have used the words *consumer* and *producer* before in a different way. In social studies, a producer is someone who makes a product. A consumer is someone who buys or uses the product.

A producer is an organism that makes its own food using sunlight, air, and water. All plants are producers. Therefore, the trees, grass, and bushes in the picture are all producers. A consumer is an organism that must eat other things for food. The mouse eats plants for food, so it is a consumer. The cat eats the mouse, so it is also a consumer.

Some consumers are **decomposers.** Decomposers break down the remains of dead organisms. They also break down animal wastes. They break down these materials into simple nutrients.

Decomposers recycle nutrients back into the soil. Plants need these nutrients to grow. Mushrooms and tiny organisms called bacteria are examples of decomposers.

Food Chains

When one organism in a habitat eats another, the first organism gains energy. The flow of energy from one organism to another can be shown in a **food chain.** All food chains start with producers.

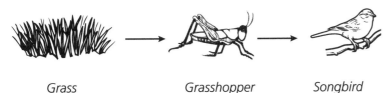

Grass   Grasshopper   Songbird

In the food chain above, a grasshopper eats grass and a songbird eats a grasshopper. Therefore, energy moves from the grass to the grasshopper. Energy moves from the grasshopper to the songbird. The grass got its energy from the Sun. The arrows in a food chain show the direction that energy flows.

A scientist is studying the consumers in a cornfield ecosystem. Which of these is the scientist not studying?

A beetles

B corn

C mushrooms

D raccoons

> The question is asking which of the choices is not a consumer. Beetles, mushrooms, and raccoons all get food from other organisms. They are all consumers. Choices A, C, and D are incorrect. Corn is a plant. It is the only organism in this group that uses sunlight to make its food. Corn is a producer, not a consumer. Choice B is correct.

All food chains start with producers. Most producers use energy from sunlight to make their food. Consumers cannot directly use energy from the Sun. They must eat producers to get energy. Without producers, consumers could not survive. Therefore, the Sun is the source of energy for most food chains on Earth.

Decomposers feed on the remains of organisms and return the useful chemical parts to the soil.

A **food chain** is a simple diagram that shows how the energy in food flows from one organism to another.

Predators and Prey

Many organisms in an ecosystem are consumers. Consumers get food by eating other organisms. Living things that capture and eat other living things are called **predators.** The organisms that predators hunt are called **prey.**

For example, red foxes are predators. They hunt and eat different kinds of prey, such as rabbits, birds, mice, and snakes. Although snakes are prey for foxes, they are also predators of other animals. Insects, mice, birds, and rabbits are prey for snakes.

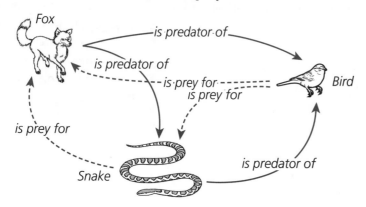

Which of the following best explains why scientists consider a lion a predator?

   A It has sharp teeth and claws.

   B It is hunted by humans.

   C It makes its own food.

   D It eats zebras and wildebeests.

Predators capture and eat living things. Choices A and B are true, but they are not what makes a lion a predator. Choice C is incorrect because it describes a producer. Choice D is the only answer that describes lions as predators, so the correct choice is D.

It's Your Turn

Please read each question carefully. For each multiple-choice question, circle the letter of the correct response.

1 **Which of these organisms is a producer?**

    A cow

    B dandelion

    C wolf

    D vulture

2 **Which of the following statements about prey is true?**

    A Other organisms eat them.

    B None of them are predators.

    C They are not part of an ecosystem.

    D They do not compete for resources.

3 **Which of these organisms helps recycle nutrients from dead plants and animals?**

    A frog

    B grass

    C bacteria

    D grasshopper

For each open-ended question, write your answers on the lines.

Base your answers to questions 4 and 5 on the food chain diagram below and on your knowledge of science.

Clover   Rabbit   Fox

4 **Identify __two__ things the clover needs to make food.**

    (1) _____

    (2) _____

5 **Explain how the fox relies on energy from the Sun.**

_____

_____

_____

Human Needs

Major Understandings 4LE5.3a, b; 4LE7.1a

Like all living things, humans have basic needs. Humans need things like water, clean air, good food, and exercise. When we get these important things, we are able to grow strong and healthy.

Humans Have Needs

You may remember that all living things share certain characteristics. For example, all living things need food. Foxes get food by hunting and eating other animals, such as mice. Trees and other plants make their own food.

Humans also need food. Every day, you probably see lots of different types of food. The food you eat at school or at home might be different from the food you can buy at a restaurant. Some foods are better for your body than other foods. For example, foods that are **unprocessed,** such as cherries, are better for your body than cherry-flavored fruit snacks. Both of those things are food, but the cherries help your body work better than the fruit snacks do.

Name <u>one</u> example of a food that is probably not good for your body. Name <u>two</u> unprocessed foods you could eat instead.

> Most foods that are very salty or very sweet are not healthy. Most foods that have a lot of fat in them are not healthy. Many processed foods contain more fat, sugar, and salt than is good for your body. Many contain chemicals that your body does not need. Potato chips and candy bars are examples of processed foods that are bad for your body. Fruits and vegetables are examples of unprocessed foods you could eat instead.

People need other things along with healthy food. Like all other living things, we need water. We also need clean air to breathe and shelter to keep us safe. If we cannot get these important things, we may become sick or even die.

Many people live in places where the air contains *pollution*. This means there are things in the air that make people sick. In some cities, people must stay inside on certain days so they don't breathe the dirty air.

Unprocessed food is food that has not been changed much from its natural state.

Eating a healthy diet does not mean that you can never eat processed or unhealthy food. You can have potato chips or a candy bar once in a while. However, you should try not to eat a lot of these foods. Make sure most of the food you eat is healthy and unprocessed.

Which of these is something all humans need to survive?

A clean water

B good music

C bright sunlight

D big houses

All of the choices are things many people want to have. But only one of them shows a human need. You can live a good, healthy life without music or a big house. Choices B and D are incorrect. Humans can live in areas of the world that get very little sunlight. Choice B is incorrect. All people need clean water. The correct answer is A.

We also need to practice **healthy habits** to keep our bodies working well. Here are some healthy habits you should have:

- Wash your hands before you eat and after you use the bathroom. When you wash your hands, you remove germs and other things that can make you sick.
- Get exercise every day. Exercise helps keep your body strong. It can even help you do better in school.
- Stay away from substances that are bad for your body. These substances include tobacco and alcohol. They also include any drugs other than ones your parents or doctor give you.

The final thing that all people need to stay healthy and strong is a good night's sleep. Every day, your body works hard. Your mind learns new things at school. Your muscles help you play sports or run outside. At the end of the day, both your body and your mind need to take a break. Sleeping helps your body and mind rest and prepare for another day.

Healthy habits are things people do to keep their bodies healthy and safe.

Most adults need about 8 hours of sleep per night. Most children and young adults need more sleep. Younger people need more sleep because their bodies are still growing.

How Humans Meet Their Needs

Like all animals, humans get food by eating other organisms. All the food people eat comes from the natural environment. Remember that some foods, such as milk and vegetables, are unprocessed. These foods have not changed much since they were grown in the natural world. But even processed foods, such as snack cakes and candy bars, are made of ingredients that came from the natural world.

As you know, all organisms including humans need shelter to survive. Look around at your school. You will see walls that are made of different materials. Some walls are made of wood. Others are made of stone. The shelters people live and work in are made of materials from the natural world. People depend on natural materials to keep them safe and warm.

Most people depend on things that other people have built. Most people in the United States do not live in homes that they built themselves. They live in homes that other people built. Your school was also probably built by a team of workers. Schools and homes are part of the **constructed** environment. Most people rely on constructed environments for shelter.

People also rely on others to provide them with good food and clean water. The fruits and vegetables you eat every day were grown by other people on a farm. Some of these farms are far away from where the food is sold. Farmers grow the food, and other people bring the food to grocery stores and schools.

In the same way, there are people who make sure the water you drink is clean. People are hard at work testing the water that comes through the pipes and into your home or school. They make sure that when you drink a glass of water, it will not make you sick.

As you can see, people are hard at work all over the world making sure other people's needs are met. Every day, you rely on both the natural environment and the constructed environment to keep your body healthy.

A **constructed** environment is an environment that people built. A house is a constructed environment.

Identify two natural items in this picture that humans need to survive. Identify one constructed item that helps meet a human need.

People use wood from trees to build their homes. Homes give them shelter. People need shelter to survive, so the trees help people survive. People also need clean water to drink. The river gives people water to help them survive. The house in the picture is a constructed item that people need. It gives people shelter.

It's Your Turn

Please read each question carefully. For each multiple-choice question, circle the letter of the correct response.

1 **Which of these could most likely help a person meet his or her basic needs?**

A   an apple

B   an owl

C   a flower

D   a toy

2 **Which of these is an example of depending on the natural environment?**

A   using an umbrella to stay dry

B   wearing a sweater to stay warm

C   eating a carrot grown in the soil

D   riding a bicycle to get from place to place

For this open-ended question, write your answers on the lines.

3 **The students in this picture are showing some unhealthy habits.**

Describe <u>two</u> healthy habits the students could do instead of the unhealthy habits.

(1) _____

(2) _____

Humans and the Environment

Major Understandings 4LE7.1b, c

Over time, people have changed Earth. They have changed environments. They have killed off many kinds of plants and animals. They have also made some positive changes. Many different human actions affect the environment.

People Harming the Environment

Most people's food comes from farms. Over time, farming has changed the environment a lot. Many of those changes have been harmful.

For example, some farmers use chemicals called **fertilizers** to help plants grow. Some farmers also use chemicals called **pesticides** to kill weeds and insects. The chemicals that farmers use can get into the water and soil. They can cause **pollution.** The pollution can harm living things.

Fertilizers are chemicals that farmers use to help their crops grow.

Pesticides are chemicals that farmers use to kill things that can harm their crops.

Pollution is any harmful substance in the environment.

The chemicals farmers spray on fields can wash into streams and rivers.

Farms can harm the environment in other ways. Many farms have a lot of animals, such as chickens or cows. The animals make a lot of wastes. The wastes can pollute the air and water.

People also change the environment by producing energy. Many people drive cars and trucks. Cars and trucks burn gasoline to get the energy they need to move. People also burn coal, oil, and natural gas to produce electricity and heat their homes. When these fuels burn, they produce air pollution. Air pollution can harm or kill plants and animals.

People also harm the environment when they **manufacture,** or make, objects. The materials people use to make these things come from the environment. For example, a company may need to dig materials such as aluminum out of the ground to make a soda can. Digging substances out of the ground can harm the environment.

To **manufacture** something is to make it out of other materials.

Chemicals from a factory flow into a stream. The stream flows to the ocean. What will most likely happen when the chemicals get to the ocean?

   A People will use them to run large ships.

   B They will make the ocean water cleaner.

   C They will kill plants and animals in the ocean.

   D Animals in the ocean will learn to use them for food.

The chemicals in the water are water pollution. People cannot use water pollution to run large ships. Choice A is incorrect. Pollution makes water dirty, not clean. Choice B is incorrect. Animals cannot use pollution for food. Choice D is incorrect. Pollution can kill plants and animals. Choice C is correct.

People also harm the environment by cutting down trees. People cut down trees so they can use the wood to make buildings and paper. They also use the forestland to build on. As a result, many animals that live in forests lose their habitats. They may become endangered or extinct. The roots of trees also help to hold soil in place. Cutting down trees can cause soil erosion. Remember that *erosion* happens when wind or water moves soil away from an area.

When people do not throw trash away properly, the trash can collect in the environment. Trash in the environment is called **litter.** Litter such as plastic bags can choke animals. If animals eat litter, they can become sick.

Litter is trash in the environment. Littering is against the law. Factories and individuals who are caught littering have to pay large fines.

People can also change the environment by building roads and parking lots. Normally, soil soaks up rainwater. When people cover the soil with roads or parking lots, the soil can't soak up the rain. The water runs off the roads and parking lots. It flows into rivers and causes floods.

Many things people do to harm the environment get worse when there are more people. Over time, the **human population** on Earth has gotten larger. The more people there are, the harder it is for everyone to meet their needs without harming the environment.

The **human population** is the number of people living on Earth.

People Helping the Environment

Some human actions help the environment. For example, **recycling** is good for the environment. It lets people use fewer materials from the environment. For example, if people recycle paper, they will not have to use as many trees to make more paper. Recycling also helps people make less trash.

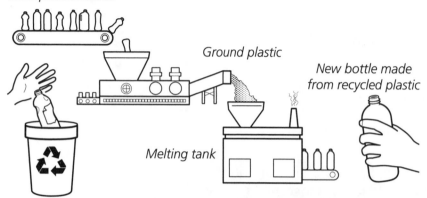

Used plastic bottles

Ground plastic

New bottle made from recycled plastic

Melting tank

Recycling plastic bottles means new products can be made from old materials.

People can protect the environment by using resources carefully. For example, people can **conserve** water by using only as much water as they need. They can conserve energy by using less electricity. Most electricity is made by burning fuels such as coal or oil. Therefore, when people use less electricity, they also use less coal and oil. By conserving, people use fewer of Earth's **natural resources.** That can help the natural resources last longer.

Some ways of helping the environment can happen only if people work together. For example, suppose people in a town want to be able to drive less. The people still need to be able to travel. If there are no buses or trains to take them places, they will still have to drive. For people in the town to drive less, the whole town needs to work together. They need to agree to get buses or trains.

A student wants to do something to help the environment. Describe <u>one</u> thing she could do by herself. Describe <u>one</u> thing she could do if she got other people to help.

An individual student can do many things to help the environment. For example, she could make sure to shut off the lights when she is not using them. If the student got others to help, she could do more. For example, her whole family could agree to keep the house cooler in the winter. That way, they would use less energy for heating.

Recycling means using old materials to make new materials.

This symbol is used around the world to mean "recycle."

To **conserve** is to use resources carefully. The act of using resources carefully is *conservation.*

Natural resources are things that exist naturally on Earth that people use to meet their needs. Natural resources include plants, animals, water, air, metals, and rocks.

It's Your Turn

Please read each question carefully. For the multiple-choice question, circle the letter of the correct response.

1 Which of these activities would probably change the environment most over time?

    A   a few people walking through the woods along a trail every year

    B   a hiker drinking water from a stream once a day

    C   a person catching three fish every week from a river

    D   a company cutting down more trees every year to make parking lots

For this open-ended question, write your answers on the lines.

2 The picture shows the result of years of environmental pollution.

Give <u>one</u> example of a human activity that probably caused the pollution. Give <u>one</u> example of a human activity that could have kept the pollution from happening.

(1) _____

(2) _____

Please read each question carefully. For each multiple-choice question, circle the letter of the correct response.

1 Which of these pictures does not show a healthy habit?

A

C

B

D

2 Spanish moss is a plant that grows from the branches of trees. It can block sunlight from reaching a tree's leaves. The moss keeps the tree from meeting its needs by stopping the tree from

A   taking in water

B   moving to a new place

C   holding itself up

D   making enough food

3 A scientist has discovered a new organism. The organism makes its own food. Other organisms eat it for food. The new organism is a

A   predator

B   consumer

C   producer

D   decomposer

UNIT 6 The Living Environment, Part 2

Base your answers to questions 4 and 5 on the diagram below and on your knowledge of science.

The diagram shows a food chain.

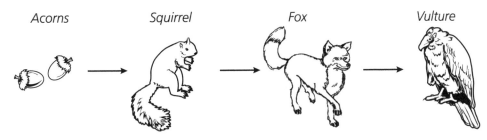

Acorns   Squirrel   Fox   Vulture

4 In this food chain, energy from the Sun flows from

  A the vulture to the fox

  B the fox to the squirrel

  C the squirrel to the acorns

  D the acorns to the squirrel

5 Which of these statements about this food chain is true?

  A The fox eats the vulture.

  B The fox eats the squirrel.

  C The squirrel eats the vulture.

  D The squirrel eats the fox.

6 Suppose all the decomposers on Earth died. What would most likely happen?

  A More plants would grow.

  B More animals would be born.

  C There would be more water for animals to drink.

  D The soil would not have enough nutrients for plants to use.

7 Cars are made of metal, plastic, rubber, and glass. It takes a lot of energy to make cars. Which of these is the most likely effect of people building cars?

  A more air and water pollution

  B more trees in forests

  C less use of coal and oil

  D less damage to ecosystems

8 People dump old tires, plastic bags, and plastic bottles into a river. How will the litter most likely affect the animals in the river?

    A They will have more food.

    B They will move to a different river.

    C Many of them will die or become sick.

    D Many of them will learn to eat the litter.

9 A student wants to be healthier. Which of these actions should the student take?

    A watch at least 1 hour of television every day

    B drink more soda for energy

    C exercise for at least 15 minutes every day

    D talk on the phone more often

For each open-ended question, write your answers on the lines.

10 In a certain field, caterpillars eat grass and robins eat caterpillars.

    Grass   *Caterpillar*   *Robin*

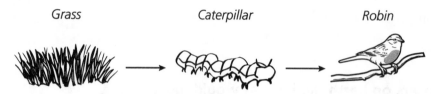

One year, a person pulls up a lot of the grass. That year, many of the robins also die. Explain why the robins died when the grass disappeared.

_____

_____

_____

11 Many people buy their milk at grocery stores. The pictures show how most milk gets to grocery stores.

| The cow is milked. | The milk is heated to destroy germs. | The milk is put into containers. | Trucks deliver the milk to stores. |

Describe <u>one</u> way people depend on the natural environment for milk. Describe <u>one</u> way they depend on the constructed environment for milk.

(1) _____

_____

(2) _____

_____